SANCTIFIED IN TRUTH

By

ANDERS BENNETT

ADISAN Publishing AB

CONTENTS

Introduction

Being a man is hard in this day and age. There is so much pressure on you. Everywhere you turn, work, deadlines, family obligations, and very little time to relax. Sometimes you may wonder how you can be pulled in so many different directions and still manage to have a close personal relationship with God. You often wonder where God is in the middle of your mess. In the Bible, Abraham, Joseph, Job, Jonah, David, and many other men endured challenging times. They made mistakes, but God was still with them and never left them.

There is nothing more important in your life than to have a relationship with Him and to keep your marriage and family focused on Him. In this 90-day devotional, you will read about many men whose lives were molded by God to do the good works He had called them to do in many spectacular ways. You will discover that He can help you follow His calling over your life. The most important thing you can do in your life is to get to know God and stay close to Him by reading your Bible and praying daily. He longs to get closer to you.

The closer you get to Him, the easier it will be for you to trust Him in the good times. It will also be even easier to stay close to Him during the challenging times of your life. Just like He delivered the men of the Bible from their troubles and taught them lessons they never forgot, He will teach you lessons that you can teach your wife, family, and even your friends. I hope this devotional teaches you to cherish your relationship with God.

Day 1
Using Your God-Given Authority

"All authority in heaven and on earth has been
given to me. Go therefore and make disciples of all
nations, baptizing them in the name of the Father and
of the Son and of the Holy Spirit, teaching them to
observe all that I have commanded you. And behold,
I am with you always, to the end of the age."
Mathew 28:18-20

One of my favorite movies is Die Hard starring Bruce Willis. He plays John McClane, a New York cop who was thrust into saving more than 30 hostages, including his wife, when terrorists, led by the infamous Hans Gruber, took over the Naka Tomi Plaza building in Los Angeles. McClane must put together all his training and use his authority as a cop to save all the hostages before it's too late. If you've seen the movie, you know that John McClane saves all the hostages and comes out victorious.

Just like John McClane used his authority as a cop, we can use the authority that God has given us whenever we face battles. With God's help, we can win the victory that God wants us to have every day of our lives. No matter what we face, God is with us and within us at all times. He has given us His divine authority to help us make the best decisions, even under stressful or uncertain circumstances. He promises to be with us always until the very end of the age.

1. How well am I using the authority that God gave me?

\
\
\
\

2. How can I use this authority to help people get closer to Him?

\
\
\
\

Dear God, thank you for giving me your divine authority to use in my life. Help me to use it to the best of my ability and not be afraid to use it every day. Help me to advance your Kingdom and to help others realize there is nothing better than having a relationship with you. In Jesus' name, amen.

DAY 2
ACCORDING TO HIS PURPOSE

*"And we know that for those who love God all
things work together for good, for those who
are called according to his purpose."*
ROMANS 8:28

My dad always said to follow my dreams. But until I was a teenager, I didn't know what my dream was. I felt like I might never amount to anything. But I eventually found out that I loved writing for God. I wanted to help others to know how a relationship with Him can change their lives. When I told my dad I wanted to write Christian articles, he said he wanted me to go after my dreams with everything I had. It hasn't always been easy but seeing the impact God has made makes it all worth it.

At times, we all ask about our purpose. We ask, "what am I supposed to do with my life?" Whether we ask ourselves or God about it, a lot of the time, it feels like we may not ever get answers. We wish the answers would flood our hearts and fill us with peace about what we are supposed to do. When we don't get the answers we want, it can be hard to remember that God made us with a special purpose. We may not find our purpose right away. It can take many years, but we will eventually find God's purpose for us. We can ask God to help us find His passions and go after them with all our hearts. Everything that God wants us to do is worth it. God works everything together for those who are called according to His purpose.

1. Have I asked God what my gifts are and how I should pursue them?

2. How can I pursue my God-given purpose?

Dear God, please help me to know what my unique gifts are and what I should do with my life. Thank you for the reminder that I am called according to your purpose. Help me to pursue my purpose to the best of my ability and to help others know you. In Jesus' name, amen.

DAY 3
GOD WILL NOT FORSAKE YOU

"The Lord will fulfill his purpose for me; your
steadfast love, O Lord, endures forever. Do
not forsake the work of your hands."
PSALM 138:8

Abraham and his wife Sarah wanted to have children. Sarah didn't think she could give Abraham a child. When Sarah heard she would have a child, she laughed and doubted God's promise. Sarah even convinced Abraham to sleep with her maidservant Hagar just so he could have a child. They knew they had made mistakes, and Abraham told Sarah to deal with Hagar the way she wanted. Even though Abraham made a mistake, God kept His promises. Abraham was 100 years old when Sarah had Isaac. When Isaac was born, they knew for certain that God had kept His promise.

We can be confident that the Lord will keep His promises to us, just like He kept His promises to Abraham. No matter what may be going on, we can come before God and literally ask Him for anything. Many of us want something from God but are afraid to ask Him because we have made mistakes. We may even be afraid to approach God because of not knowing how He will react to us. No matter the mistakes we have made, God still loves us. Rather than being afraid to approach God with our needs and wants, we can come to Him anytime, day or night. He gladly listens to us whether we pray, vent, scream, or sob. We can be confident that the Lord will fulfill His purpose. He will not forsake the work of His hands.

1. How well have I approached God about anything I need in my life?

____

____

____

____

2. How can I help others in my life believe in their God-given purpose?

____

____

____

____

Dear God, please help me to believe that you have wonderful plans for my life. Thank you that I can come to you for any and every reason, no matter what my needs or wants are. Help me to find what my purpose is and to pursue it with the passion you placed inside me when you created me. Thank you for never forsaking me. In Jesus' name, amen.

Day 4

Fulfilling His Purpose

"I cry out to God Most High, to God
who fulfills his purpose for me."
Psalm 57:2

My daughter was born three months early and had a stroke at birth. The doctors didn't expect her to live even a month. She was one pound nine ounces at birth. They didn't think she could see, hear, walk, or talk normally. They also told my wife and me to start preparing for my daughter to be mentally and physically handicapped. When the nurses called us the day after Thanksgiving to say that we needed to say goodbye to her, I cried out to God. I begged Him to let my daughter live. I made a deal with Him. If He let my daughter live, I'd surrender my life to Him. He was faithful and let my daughter live without physical or mental handicaps. I have a strong relationship with Him and love how He has made my daughter and me close. I know God will fulfill His purpose for her life.

Just like this man cried out to God to protect and save his daughter, we, too, can cry out to Him whenever we need Him. We can cry out to Him when we want one-on-one time with Him. There is nothing that He won't do for us, and there is nothing that He can't do in our lives. If He can save this man's daughter, imagine what He can do for us in our lives. All we have to do is be brave enough to ask Him for His help.

1. What is God's purpose for me, and have I been pursuing it correctly?

____

____

____

____

____

2. How can I pursue God's purpose for my life in a way that brings glory to Him?

____

____

____

____

____

Dear God, thank you for letting me come to you no matter what may be happening in my life. Thank you for always listening to me. Help me to find my purpose and pursue it in a way that brings glory to you throughout my life. In Jesus' name, amen.

Day 5

He Began a Good Work in You

"And I am sure of this, that he who began a good work in
you will bring it to completion at the day of Jesus Christ."
Philippians 1:6

In the Bible, when Joseph was betrayed by his brothers and sold into slavery, most likely, Joseph didn't understand what God's plan was for his life. All he could feel was anger and utter despair after being enslaved when he originally never had to work a day in his life. Even when he got a better position with Potiphar, his wife tried to say that Joseph made sexual advances on her and had him put in jail. While in jail, Joseph interpreted two prisoners' dreams, both of which were correct. Just when Joseph thought his life would be turned around, he was dealt another blow when the prisoner didn't tell Pharaoh about his ability to interpret dreams as soon as Joseph wanted him to. Joseph waited 13 years to be released from prison. But God had an awesome plan and purpose for Him.

Just like Joseph, we can doubt that God will fulfill His plans for our lives when things don't happen when we want them to. It feels like God isn't even listening to us. But the exact opposite is true. God hears us at all times and is working behind the scenes of our lives even when we feel ignored by Him. Just like Joseph must have felt ignored by God, we often forget that God will fulfill His purpose in our lives. But God is always fulfilling His purpose for our lives in ways that only He can, just like He did with Joseph.

1. How can I be sure and believe that God will fulfill His purpose for my life?

____

____

____

____

2. How have I been pursuing God's plan and purpose in my life?

____

____

____

____

Dear God, please help me to believe in your purpose for my life. Thank you for starting a good work in my life and for reminding me that you will bring it to completion, but in your timing and your ways. Help me to trust you more and more each day. In Jesus' name, amen.

Day 6
Who Am I?

"But Moses said to God, "Who am I that I should
go to Pharaoh and bring the Israelites out of
Egypt?" And God said, "I will be with you..."
Exodus 3:11-12

Moses experienced fear and uncertainty in his life, especially when God appeared to him in the burning bush. He didn't understand who God was even after He said, "I am that I am." God had to explain that He was the God of his ancestors, Abraham, Isaac, and Jacob. Moses was afraid of God. When Moses heard that God had handpicked him to lead the Israelites out of Egypt, he scoffed at God, telling Him that He had picked the wrong guy. Moses thought that there was no way he could lead the Israelites out of slavery. God knew Moses was afraid of the task He asked him to do. But God reassured Moses that He would be with him and teach him what to say when he went to Egypt. He reassured Moses that He would strengthen him.

Many times, we feel the same way Moses felt. We are often filled with uncertainty, fear, and anxiety when God asks us to do something. We automatically cower, saying, "Me? Who am I that you want me to do this task? How can I do it?" Then God reassures us that He will strengthen us for the task ahead. We can rest assured that He will never tell us to do something without first enabling us to do it. If He can equip Moses with the right words to say, surely, He will strengthen us and equip us with the right things to say and do in any situation.

1. How have I been like Moses and doubted I could do what God told me to do?

____

____

____

____

____

2. How can I stand up in faith and say that I can do whatever task God wants me to do?

____

____

____

____

____

____

Dear God, whenever I have trouble believing that you equipped me to do something, please reassure me that you will be with me, just like you did for Moses. Please strengthen me for everything that you have called me to do. Let me walk out in faith and believe that I'm doing everything for your glory. In Jesus' name, amen.

Day 7
I Can Do All Things

Moses thought he could never lead the Israelites out of slavery. But God was already working in his life in ways only He could. Moses was bad at speaking in public. He stuttered a lot. No wonder he thought he wasn't the right one to help the Israelites. Even though Moses doubted himself, God knew He had picked the right person for the job. God then reassured Moses that He would be with him in every situation. He even told Moses exactly what to say when he went to Egypt. After that, Moses began to believe that God had given him the strength to do the task, even if it was daunting.

We often think, like Moses, that we are limited by our abilities or, even more so, by our disabilities. Moses was a stutterer, and he thought that meant he couldn't talk to the Israelites or reason with Pharaoh. But God didn't let that stop Moses from fulfilling His plan. He allowed Moses to speak in His ways so that the people would know that it was God speaking through him. The great news is that God allows us to lead our families in the way of the Lord, just as Moses did. Whenever we think we can't do something, we can push those doubts out of our minds and remember that we can do everything through Christ, who gives us strength. There's nothing we can't do with God's help.

1. Do I really believe that I can do all things through Christ who gives me strength?

____

____

____

____

____

2. In what ways can I remind myself that I can accomplish any task, big or small, with God's help?

____

____

____

____

____

Dear God, thank you for giving me your strength for everyday tasks. Thank you for teaching me how to obtain your strength, no matter what I may be facing. Please help me to be a Godly father and husband and to lead my family in your ways. Thank you for everything that you have equipped me to do. Help me to do things to the best of my ability and for your glory. In Jesus' name, amen.

Day 8
Waiting for The Lord

"But they who wait for the Lord shall renew their strength;
they shall mount up with wings like eagles; they shall
run and not be weary; they shall walk and not faint."
Isaiah 40:31

Men often want to do everything in their own specific ways and in their own times. Many men in the Bible did things without God at the forefront of their lives. For example, David had an affair with Uriah's wife, Bathsheba. Abraham had an affair with his wife's maidservant, Hagar. Joseph wanted to divorce Mary when he found out she was pregnant with Jesus through immaculate conception. Jonah ran away from God when He told Jonah to go to Nineveh to tell the people there that God was about to destroy their city. All those men made their own choices instead of asking God what He wanted them to do in their lives. Soon, they lost their strength and stamina because they turned away from God. The good news is that God never turned His back on them and strengthened them for their journeys ahead.

We lead ourselves astray and forget to talk to God, asking Him to give us the patience and ability to wait for Him to tell us which ways we should go. We can learn that when we wait on the Lord, we will get clear guidance about the direction of our lives, no matter how long it takes. When we learn to listen to God instead of ourselves, He will renew our strength and help us soar through life like eagles. With God's help, we can run and not be weary and walk and not faint.

1. Have I given my life and everyday activities over to the Lord?

2. What are some ways that I can remember to wait for Him to work on and in my everyday life?

Dear God, please help me to let go of the reigns of my life and turn to you. Help me to wait for you to tell me where to go and what to do. Help me to want to do what you've asked me to do with a grateful heart. Thank you for renewing my strength and allowing me to wait on your promises. In Jesus' name, amen.

Day 9

God is My Portion

"My flesh and my heart may fail, but God is the strength of my heart and my portion forever."
Psalm 73:26

I have struggled with severe back pain since I was in my mid-forties. I have prayed over and over for my back pain to be relieved and fully taken away. Sometimes I get discouraged and wonder if God even hears me when I pray. I also wonder where He is when my back pain gets severe. I try not to sink too far into despair because I know my pain and mental focus will only worsen. Whenever I lose my focus on God, He always gives me a nudge to tell me that He is still working on and in my life. I realize that even though my heart and my flesh may hurt and fail me, no matter what, God has never failed me. Not once. And He never will.

Just as this man prayed for his back pain to be healed, whenever we go through hard times and feel discouraged, that is where God taps us on the shoulder and tells us that He is still right there with us even when we are in pain. We can rest assured that no matter our physical, mental, emotional, or even spiritual ailments, God is our strength and our portion forever. There is nothing He won't do for us and within our lives. God has never made a mistake in the way He has created us. Even though we may not like our bodies, we can embrace ourselves because God made us.

1. How have I felt like my body, mind, or spirit was failing me?

____

____

____

____

____

2. How has God shown me that He made my body perfect and that He will never fail me?

____

____

____

____

____

Dear God, please help me to trust that you made my body in your perfect way. Teach me to remember that even though I might have pain in certain areas of my body, mind, or soul, you will sustain me and help me through it. Thank you that you are my strength and portion forever. In Jesus' name, amen.

DAY 10
TRUE MAN OF GOD

"The Lord is my strength and my shield; in him my
heart trusts, and I am helped; my heart exults,
and with my song I give thanks to him."
PSALM 28:7

David was a true man of God in every sense of the word. He defeated the giant Goliath when he was a young boy with only a few round stones and a sling. He stood up when people said he couldn't defeat Goliath and told them that God would help him defeat Goliath. He became king of Israel at only 30 years old. But David was not perfect by any means. He also made mistakes because he was human and sinned, just like all of us. David had many scary experiences in his life, including when King Saul pursued him and attempted to kill him because Saul was jealous of him. But through it all, David clung to the hope he found in God. The Lord was his strength and shield. David knew he had to keep trusting in God even through difficult circumstances.

We, too, are humans and make mistakes daily, just like David did. We can trust God whenever we go through hard times. When we trust in God, it focuses on our problems and on the one who can help us through the hard times. It turns our anguish into worship. When we turn away from the doubt in our hearts and turn our trust to God, He helps us in ways we never thought possible. We can learn to give thanks to Him in every and any situation.

1. How have I learned to trust God in my life?

____

____

____

____

____

2. In what ways can I put my trust in God into action?

____

____

____

____

____

Dear God, please help me to remember that you can help me through anything. Thank you for the help that you've given to me throughout my life. Thank you that I can give thanks to you for anything and everything. Please remind me that no matter how hard things get that I can rejoice in the hope I have found in you. Please help me become a true man of God. In Jesus' name, amen.

Day 11

Ultimate Kindness

*"For this very reason, make every effort to supplement
your faith with virtue, and virtue with knowledge."*
2 Peter 1:5

Another one of my favorite movies is Shrek. In that movie, the donkey, played by Eddie Murphy, tries to befriend the angry ogre Shrek. Shrek doesn't want to be friends with Donkey because he is so annoying. But throughout the movie, Donkey does everything he can to try and be friends with Shrek, even though Shrek resists Donkey's friendliness. Even when Shrek tells him to get lost, Donkey stays by his side, trying to prove his loyalty to Shrek. Shrek then admitted to Donkey that everyone judged him before they knew him, which was why he wanted to be alone. Shrek then realizes that Donkey really is his true friend. He also realizes that even though they have different lifestyles and opinions about things, they both can still treat each other with kindness.

The same thing applies to our friendships with the people in our lives. Even though we can and will have different opinions about topics in life, we can still be kind to our friends, wives, and children. Just like it says in this verse, to keep our faith and kindness at the center of our lives, we men can learn a thing or two from Shrek and Donkey's friendship. We can learn to be loyal to the people we love despite our differences. We can act and speak lovingly in our faith walk towards everyone in our lives.

1. How have I shown my family and friends loyalty?

____

____

____

____

____

2. How can I show kindness through my faith walk?

____

____

____

____

____

Dear God, please help me to show kindness and to share my faith with anyone who needs encouragement. Thank you for the people in my life that let me know they are truly my friends. Thank you for always being there for me and for always being loyal to me, Lord. Thank you for allowing me to be kind to everyone I meet. Please help me to walk boldly in my faith walk. In Jesus' name, amen.

Day 12
Think about Good Things

"Finally, brothers, whatever is true, whatever is honorable,
whatever is just, whatever is pure, whatever is lovely,
whatever is commendable, if there is any excellence, if there
is anything worthy of praise, think about these things."
Philippians 4:8

David was a man who gave praise to God no matter what. He praised God through hard and good times. Abraham kept the faith and did what God told him to do when he was told to build the ark. Moses did what he was afraid to do by telling Pharoah to let the Israelites go free from slavery in Egypt. All of these men meditated on what God was telling them to do. They meditated on God's words and brought about some amazing changes in human history. David was eventually the king of Israel and loved God with all his heart. Abraham became the father of many nations, and Moses saved his people.

We don't have to automatically keep thinking about any destructive thoughts that come into our minds. God calls us to meditate on His words and think of anything true, honorable, just, pure, lovely, commendable, excellent, and praiseworthy. We have control over what we think. We can control how we react to any news in our lives. We can be like David, Abraham, and Moses and think of ways to help others come to know the goodness of God. Think about it. David, Abraham, and Moses each participated in amazing events in history. Now it is our chance to see how we can help make our Godly mark on history by doing what God tells us to do.

1. Am I meditating on what God has told me to do in my life?

____

____

____

____

____

2. How can I make my mark and change the world for the better with God's help?

____

____

____

____

____

Dear God, please help me to think about what you want me to think about. Help me to meditate on anything that makes you happy. Thank you for giving me the chance to think about anything that is true, honorable, just, pure, lovely, commendable, excellent, or praiseworthy. Help me to show others how to meditate on your word every day through my words and actions. In Jesus' name, amen.

Day 13
You Did It for Me

"And the King will answer them, 'Truly, I say to you, as you did it to one of the least of these my brothers, you did it to me.'
Mathew 25:40

Jesus was and is the most selfless man on earth. He was created to help people and save them. He was willing to do anything and everything to help the people who needed it the most, whether they were men, women, children, young or old. He didn't care whether they were tax collectors, wealthy people, or poor people. He just wanted to help people and to let them know that the only way to heaven was through faith in Him. He was not afraid to heal the sick or wounded or to visit people who needed Him the most when they were grieving the loss of a loved one. There was nothing He wouldn't do for people, including dying on the cross.

We can learn a great lesson from Jesus. He says whatever we do for the people in our lives, out of love and in the goodness of our hearts, we do it for Him. So, whenever we open the door for a stranger, help someone carry groceries to their car, spend time with our sons or daughters by playing with them outside, or spend some much-needed one-on-one time with our spouse, we do it for Jesus. Whenever we listen to a friend going through a hard time without giving them advice, we are being the hands and feet of Jesus by helping them know that they are not alone.

1. Am I helping people the way God instructed me to help them?

____

____

____

____

____

2. How can I be more like Jesus in my thoughts, words, and my actions to-
    wards people?

____

____

____

____

____

Dear God, please help me to want to help others out in the same way that you help them. Thank you for always being willing to help me, whatever my needs are. Please lead me to know when to just sit and listen whenever someone is in need of my listening ear. Help me to be there for people the way that you are there for me. In Jesus' name, amen.

Day 14

Full Reward

> *"The* Lord *repay you for what you have done, and a full reward be given you by the* Lord*, the God of Israel, under whose wings you have come to take refuge!"*
> Ruth 2:12

Boaz was very pleased with what Ruth had done for her mother-in-law, and he said to her that the Lord would repay her for her goodness. Boaz was a man of God. He was also a man of honor and integrity. He eventually asked Ruth to marry him and kept her husband's last name to maintain the dead's name within his property. Boaz did the right thing when he married Ruth because he gave her a second chance at having a normal life and a family. He knew she was a true woman of God and had taken refuge under God. He knew that she was to be honored, respected, and treated fairly.

We can learn how to treat the women in our lives through Boaz's example, whether they are our children, mothers, friends, coworkers, and especially our wives. We can treat them in the same tender, Godly way that Boaz treated Ruth. We can treat our wives with the honor, respect, and love that they deserve every day of their lives, no matter what. Whenever we go through hard times in our marriage, we can ask God to help us remember what made us fall in love with our wives in the first place. We can also ask Him to show us how to love our wives in the way He loves them daily.

1.   Am I loving my wife in a way that honors her and God?

____

____

____

____

____

2.   How can I show my wife that I love her the same way God loves her?

____

____

____

____

____

Dear God, please help me to love my wife the way that you love her. Thank you for helping me fall in love with her and for our marriage. Please help me to remember what drew us together in the first place whenever times get tough for us. Help me to love and respect her in the way that she needs to be loved and respected.

Day 15

Walk in Integrity

"Whoever walks in integrity walks securely, but he who makes his ways crooked will be found out."
Proverbs 10:9

Job was one of the most integrity-filled men in the Bible. Despite what went on in his life, he didn't sin or turn away from God even when his own family told him to. He kept praising God despite his circumstances and never wavered in his faith. Nothing that happened to him could ever shake his faith. If anything, his circumstances only strengthened his faith and belief in God. They brought him closer to God, which surprised everyone in his life. He walked with integrity every day of his life and walked securely in his faith. If you've read Job, you know God rewarded Job for his unwavering faith.

Job's faith saw him through the most difficult circumstances. Luckily, we are blessed, and we can have our faith see us through any and all circumstances. We can learn how to be men of integrity by reading Job's story. We don't have to walk away from God when hard times come upon us because we know deep in our hearts, just like Job did, that there's no way we can even make it in our lives without God. Even though we sometimes make mistakes and turn away from God, we always realize that we are nothing without Him. Our faith is the most important part of our lives.

1. Am I living my life with integrity?

____

____

____

____

____

2. How can I live my life with some of the same integrity that Job had?

____

____

____

____

____

Dear God, please help me to live my life with integrity no matter what comes my way. Please help me to live out my faith walk with honor and to help others know you through my thoughts, words, and actions. Thank you for helping me realize that I am nothing without you in my life. In Jesus' name, amen.

Day 16
I Made It with God

> "Brothers, I do not consider that I have made it my own.
> But one thing I do: forgetting what lies behind and straining
> forward to what lies ahead, I press on toward the goal
> for the prize of the upward call of God in Christ Jesus."
> PHILIPPIANS 3:13-14

Paul, the apostle, said he knew he didn't make it through his difficult journey alone. He knew God was with him no matter what. Think about it for a minute. Did you know that Paul was originally Saul? He hated Christians, persecuted them, and even killed them for following Jesus. Everyone lived in complete fear of him. But, while he was on the way to Damascus, God caused him to fall to the ground and struck him blind. Jesus then spoke to him, asking him, "Saul, Saul, why do you persecute me?" Saul asked him, "who are you?" Jesus replied, "I am Jesus the one you are persecuting…" (Acts 9:1-22) If you know the story, you know Jesus changed Saul's heart and made him one of the Godliest men in the Bible. He told people to continue to press onward towards their goals from God.

We have to remind ourselves that we don't make it alone, but we only make it with God's help. He gives us the goals that are in our hearts. But so often, we think that we make it on our own. Rather than remembering to thank God for giving us the goals in our hearts, we think that we accomplish things on our own. It doesn't do us any good to remember our past. He wants us to press towards the goal of the prize and follow His call on our lives as husbands, fathers, brothers, uncles, nephews, and friends.

1. Am I pressing on towards the goals of my life with God at the forefront of my mind?

____

____

____

____

2. How can I press on toward God's goals for my life instead of thinking about what lies behind me?

____

____

____

____

Dear God, please help me to forget the things of my past and to press on towards the goals that you have put in my heart for my future. Help me to press on towards the prize that is my victory through you, Lord! Thank you for helping me to experience the calling that you have placed in my life and for helping me overcome my past. Thank you for your amazing call over my life and for your magnificent plan for my life. Help me to embrace you every day. In Jesus' name, amen.

DAY 17
ALL THINGS ARE POSSIBLE

"But Jesus looked at them and said, "With man this is
impossible, but with God all things are possible."
MATHEW 19:26

David was a shepherd out in the field way before God anointed him as king over Israel. He was small in stature, and no one thought he would amount to much. His father, Jesse, told him to go to his brothers who were at war with the Philistines and bring them lunch. There was a huge warrior named Goliath threatening the other men. When David saw the soldiers cowering in fear because of Goliath, he made up his mind that he was going to fight Goliath with God's help. Even when the king and his family said that David wouldn't be able to fight nonetheless defeat Goliath, David had faith in God that he would succeed. David struck Goliath with smooth stones, fell to the ground, and died. See, with God, David could defeat Goliath.

In this chapter of Mathew, the disciples asked Jesus who could be saved. They thought that it was literally impossible for people to be saved. Suppose God could anoint David to defeat Goliath with three small stones and help David have the faith of a warrior of Christ. In that case, we can realize that we can defeat any giant that comes our way. We can teach our kids and wives how to be warriors of Christ. We can be men that are warriors against the flesh and cling to God in every area of our lives.

1. Do I really believe that all things are possible through Christ?

____

____

____

____

____

2. How can I help others realize that all things are possible with God and that they can be saved?

____

____

____

____

____

Dear God, when things get difficult, please help me to believe that I can get through anything and everything with your help. Help me to believe that all things are possible through you. Help me to trust in you no matter what happens in my life. Let me help others believe that there is nothing they can't get through with you at their side. In Jesus' name, amen.

Day 18
Grow in Grace and Knowledge of God

Peter was a man who made mistakes, but Jesus still called him one of His disciples. He told Jesus that He would never go to the cross and that He would never die a death for all of us on earth. When Jesus told Peter to get behind Him, Peter must have been crushed. Jesus also told Peter he would deny Him three times before the rooster crowed. Peter didn't believe Him. Peter ended up denying Jesus three times and was ashamed of what he had done because Jesus was his closest friend. When he saw that Jesus was no longer in the grave, he was full of sorrow. Yet, when Jesus appeared to him in the locked room upstairs, he knew that Jesus had forgiven his sins.

At times, we as men think we know everything there is to know in our lives, just like Peter did. So often, when we think like that, God gets our attention with the snap of His fingers. God doesn't want us to think that we know everything. Rather He wants us to grow in the grace and knowledge of Jesus Christ and what He can do in our marriage, family life, friend's circle, and even work. There is always something to learn about Jesus. We must also remember that there is much we can learn about ourselves. Whatever we do, we can grow in our knowledge of God every day.

1. Am I allowing myself to grow in the grace and knowledge of Christ?

____

____

____

____

____

2. Do I give Him the glory He rightfully deserves every day?

____

____

____

____

____

Dear God, please help me to grow in the grace, truth, and knowledge of you in every area of my life. Please show me how I need to grow in my knowledge of you every day. Help me to reach out to others and let them know that there is nothing more important than knowing you as their Lord and Savior. In Jesus' name, amen.

Day 19
The Lord Directs Your Steps

"In their hearts humans plan their course,
but the Lord establishes their steps."
Proverbs 16:9

Jonah was told by God to go to Nineveh and warn the people that God was about to destroy them because of their sins. Instead of listening to God, Jonah went away from Nineveh because he was afraid of the people. He went to another land and then got on a boat. On the way to another port, a storm started. If you've ever read the story of Jonah, you know that he told the men that he'd disobeyed God. He told the men to throw him into the sea, and the storm would stop. Jonah was swallowed by a whale and then spit out. He then went to Nineveh to tell the people to stop sinning. God healed the Ninevites' hearts, and they worshiped Him.

All men can learn from Jonah. When the Lord tells us to do something, we'd better do it. We might have plans for how our lives will go, but we know that things can change instantly. Whenever God wants us to help save someone's life, whether, in our family or friend's circle, we should do everything we can to tell them about God. We can go where God is leading us even if it scares us or makes us uncomfortable. Jonah went where God was leading him to go only after being in a storm and swallowed by a whale. Doing what God tells us to do the first time is always a better option.

1. Am I allowing God to establish His paths for my life?

2. How can I let go and allow God to take the reigns of my life?

Dear God, please help me to give you the reigns of my life instead of trying to do everything on my own. Please help me to remember that your plans are much better than mine ever could be. Thank you for establishing the steps of my life before I was even born. Thank you for placing your hand over every aspect of my life. Help me to teach others to give up control of their lives and to let you have control. In Jesus' name, amen.

Day 20

Never Give Up

"But as for you, be strong and do not give
up, for your work will be rewarded."
2 Chronicles 15:7

My daughter was in physical and occupational therapy for 14 years. As a child, she didn't understand why she had to go to therapy, but she never complained. She went into every session with determination and came out of every session stronger physically and mentally than when she went in. I admired her courage in the face of adversity because the things her therapists asked her to do were very difficult for a child her age. The day she was released from therapy, she felt like a huge weight had been lifted. I admired her strength, courage, and never give up attitude during those difficult times. Whenever I see her getting discouraged, I remind her of how far she has come because of her never give up attitude. Her hard work was rewarded by God.

Just like this man learned a lot from his daughter, we, too, can learn to never give up no matter how hard times are. God will reward our hard work if we can learn to never give up on ourselves or our goals. Jesus will help us to keep going no matter what. Even if we are struggling, we can turn to God and say, "Lord, I need your help to get through this. Please guide me in the right direction." Once we give our lives over to God and tell ourselves not to give up when we go through troubles, we will become even stronger.

1. In what ways have I given up my goals in my life and focused on God's plan for my life?

____

____

____

____

____

2. What can I do to remain strong when reaching for my goals?

____

____

____

____

____

Dear God, please help me to never give up on the goals that you have placed in my heart. Please help me to remember that my work for you will always be rewarded. Help me to stay strong in the face of adversity and to turn to you for your strength. Thank you that you are always with me when I'm trying to achieve any goals. In Jesus' name, amen.

Day 21
Come Before God

Paul gave all people specific instructions on how we can worship. He wants every man to pray, lifting their hands without any anger in their heart and without quarreling with people in their life. He gave men these specific instructions as to how they should pray. They should pray at any time, wherever they are, and lift their hands to God without anger or quarreling. Paul said that God doesn't want men to come before Him in prayer if they have grievances against or quarreling with people. Men can come before God no matter where they are or what they are doing and immerse themselves in prayer before Him as their holy God and the King of Kings.

Paul wants all men to know they don't have to be afraid or nervous to come before God. Even though we sin every day, the good news is that God still loves us no matter what. Sometimes, we won't want to approach God because of our sins. But often, when we don't feel worthy enough to approach God, that's when we need to come before Him with all of our flaws, mistakes, burdens, and cares. Instead of fear, we can come before Him in happy, true, reverent worship. We can come before God whether we need something or not. We should be willing to praise Him no matter what happens in our lives.

1. Am I lifting my hands in worship, or am I finding the time to quarrel with those around me?

____

____

____

____

____

2. Have I made time to pray wherever I am in my life?

____

____

____

____

____

Dear God, please help me to lift up my hands in prayer wherever I am. Thank you for the ability to praise you whenever I can and wherever I am. Please help me to turn to you in prayer in every situation, and please help me to be the light in the broken world. Help me to teach the men around me to pray for and with each other. In Jesus' name, amen.

Day 22

Lead Me in Your Ways

"But I want you to understand that the head of
every man is Christ, the head of a wife is her
husband, and the head of Christ is God."
1 Corinthians 11:3

In the first year of our marriage, it was very difficult. My wife and I worked shifts opposite each other, so we barely saw each other. But when we did see each other, we had to learn to live with each other 24 hours a day. I realize now that I had to learn to love my wife the way God loves her. I had to let my walls down and trust my wife in a way that let her know that it was ok for her to trust me completely too. God helped me embrace her the same way He embraces her. I saw her in a whole new light. God allowed me to lead her in ways that can only come from Him.

Paul again offered men advice that they are the leaders of their households. The head of every man is Christ Himself. All men are the head of their households, families, and marriages. We are to lead our families in the love and the structure of the Lord. We can ask Him how we can be married and in love with our wives. As long as we lead with God at the forefront of our marriage, there is nothing we can't do for and with our wives as a team. Whenever we go through low points in our marriages, we can remember that God gave us the ability to lead our marriages in His ways.

1. Am I walking around like I am a true believer in God?

2. How can I be like Christ and be a leader in my marriage?

Dear God, please teach me how to be a leader for you in my marriage. Please help me to lead my wife in love. Help me to live in love as you have loved me. Teach me how to love my wife the way that you love her. Thank you for being the head of my heart and my life. Thank you for changing my life and our marriage for the best. In Jesus' name, amen.

Day 23

Love Your Wife As God Does

"For the husband is the head of the wife even as Christ
is the head of the church, his body, and is himself
its Savior. Husbands, love your wives, as Christ
loved the church and gave himself up for her."
Ephesians 5:25

I realized early on in my marriage that God wanted me to honor my wife in different ways. He wanted me to honor her in how I talked to her and interacted with her, and He wanted me to help her in her everyday struggles. I knew it would take God working in my life and heart to love my wife the same way God loves me. I had to put away my pride and say, "I know that I make mistakes as much as she does." I know I need God to open my eyes and heart to learn how to approach her the way God approaches me. Over the years, God has shown me how to lead and love her in new and exciting ways every week.

All men can learn from this man's example. The head of every marriage is the husband. Instead of walking or running away from the calling that God has for our lives, we can embrace our roles as husbands and the leaders of our families. We can approach our wives with the same love that God gives us and try our best to have the same level of understanding that God has for us. It is our biggest calling to show our wives who Christ is. In the same way, we show ourselves who Christ is and what He can be in our lives and our marriages.

1. Am I acting like I am the head of my household or letting God be the head of my household?

2. How can I love my wife just as God loves her?

Dear God, please help me be a leader in my life and in my marriage. Help me to be the head of my marriage through the gifts and the abilities that you gave me each and every day. Help me to love my wife in the way that you love her and to lead her in your ways every day of our marriage. In Jesus' name, amen.

Day 24
Prayers of Intercession

"First of all, then, I urge that supplications, prayers, intercessions, and thanksgivings be made for all people, for kings and all who are in high positions, that we may lead a peaceful and quiet life, godly and dignified in every way."
1 Timothy 2:1-2

Praying for people is the best thing that I can do. No matter what I'm doing or where I am, I can stop and pray for everyone around me. If I see someone struggling, I ask them if I can pray for them and let them know that I'm continuing to lift them up in prayer. Prayer changes everything. It brings me peace even in the most difficult situations. It turns my focus from the problem to the One who can and will fix every problem. I encourage people to just start praying for others and watch how their life changes. Remember, there is nothing that God doesn't hear when we pray. He hears us when we cry, are angry, or are even desperate. We can learn to live a prayer-filled life and see how our lives change when we lead dignified and Godly lives.

Just like this man prays for the people in his life, we too can approach God's throne anytime, anywhere, and come to Him. We can pray for the people in our lives, the restoration of our marriages, our family lives, and our church leaders. We can even pray for the leaders of the world that they see God move in mighty ways in their individual lives and in their work. He wants us to come before Him interceding on people's behalf with thanksgiving. Through Him, we can lead Godly lives.

1. In what ways am I praying for the people in my life?

____

____

____

____

2. How can I lead a peaceful, kind, quiet, and Godly life?

____

____

____

____

Dear God, please help me to lead a life that is completely focused on you and to live a life that is pleasing to you. Please help me to pray for the leaders of our nation and for them to be brought to the knowledge of you in everything they do. Help me to pray for everyone around me. Thank you for allowing me to learn to be dignified in every way through my relationship with you. In Jesus' name, amen.

Day 25

Manage Your Household with Dignity

"He must manage his own household well, with all dignity keeping his children submissive, for if someone does not know how to manage his own household, how will he care for God's church?"
1 Timothy 3:4

Being a father is one of the best yet most demanding and difficult positions we can ever be put in as a man. It can wear us out in the best and worst ways. But Paul encourages all fathers to raise children with dignity and to keep our children submissive unto God. He also says to raise our children in the love of Christ. Managing our households is one of the most important jobs we can ever have as husbands and fathers. We will fail daily, but God will help us live with humility.

Managing our household is tough at times. We sin daily and make mistakes in how we interact with our children. We yell at them, spank them, and send them to their rooms for not doing things the way we want them done. We also argue about what is best for our children, no matter how old they are, which causes even more strife between them and us. We must be the first to approach our children and ask for their forgiveness whenever we mess up. We can come to our children and tell them, "I'm sorry. I messed up, and I hope you can forgive me. I am only trying to help you avoid making the same mistakes I made at your age."

1. Am I managing my household with peace and dignity and in the ways God wants me to?

____

____

____

____

____

2. How can I change my life and attitude about raising my household in a way that pleases God?

____

____

____

____

____

Dear God, please help me to raise my children in your ways, not my ways. Please help me to keep my eyes focused on you in my marriage. Please help me to know how to walk with you in everything I do and speak. Thank you for giving me the ability to manage my household in your name every day. In Jesus' name, amen.

Day 26
Enduring All Things

"Love is patient and kind; love does not envy or boast; it is not arrogant or rude. It does not insist on its own way; it is not irritable or resentful; it does not rejoice at wrongdoing, but rejoices with the truth. Love bears all things, believes all things, hopes all things, endures all things."
1 Corinthians 13:4-7

My girlfriend and I went to a Christian concert years ago. She invited one of her best friends to come with us. She had always wanted to take her friend to a Christian concert, and I knew that she only had that one chance. I ended up giving him my seat, and I sat in his seat a few rows up so he could sit with her at the concert. I did it for my girlfriend so she would be happy. Before the concert, I talked to God about what He wanted me to do and realized that I would most likely have to give up my seat for the other guy. So I followed God's directions. It was very difficult to give up my seat, but I knew it made my girlfriend happy. It made me realize how much I loved my girlfriend. I did what God told me to do and felt unconditional love for my girlfriend.

Even though this man didn't want to give up his seat at the concert, he realized how important it was for his girlfriend to sit by her friend. He willingly gave up his seat for her and showed unconditional love for his girlfriend. He proved that love is patient and kind and that it bears and endures all things. Even though there are things we don't want to do in our relationships, God will give us a way through them.

1. Am I willing to give up my seat for someone else and do what God has called me to do?

____

____

____

____

____

2. Can I give up my seat at a concert or other event in order to help someone else?

____

____

____

____

____

Dear God, please help me to realize that your unconditional love is what can carry us through even when we don't want to go through a hard situation. Help me to be willing to give up my seat for others. Thank you for your unconditional love. Please help me to let others know that you are covering them with your unconditional love. In Jesus' name, amen.

Day 27
Covers a Multitude

*"Above all, keep loving one another earnestly,
since love covers a multitude of sins."*
1 Peter 4:8

My girlfriend was struggling with realizing that a friend from her past wasn't good for her mental health. She didn't want to hear that he didn't care about her. She did anything to keep the friendship going. This continued for eight years, starting four years before God brought us together. I didn't know what to do besides praying for her to see the truth. I asked God whether I should stay or walk away from her. But God clearly told me, "She needs you to get through this because she has been hurt many times before." I continued to pray and believe that God would open her eyes. One day she called me and told me she was done being friends with the other guy. I thought it wasn't true, but that night she hugged me and started crying, asking for forgiveness for not realizing the truth sooner. I told her I forgave her, and I knew God changed her heart and helped her realize that she always was and is worth so much more.

Just like this man forgave his girlfriend for making the wrong choice with a friend, we can forgive our girlfriends or wives for their sins and completely forget them in the same way God does. There is no sin that He can't cover. There is nothing He can't help us through and nothing He won't do for us in our lives and marriages.

1. Do I believe that love covers a multitude of sins?

____

____

____

____

____

2. How can I continue to receive God's unconditional love for me?

____

____

____

____

____

Dear God, please help me to realize that your unconditional love covers a multitude of sins. Thank you for your unconditional love. Please help me to let others know that you can and are covering them with your unconditional love. Please help me to forgive people quickly, just as you forgive me every day. Thank you that your love covers a multitude of sins. In Jesus' name, amen.

Day 28

Laying Down Our lives

"By this we know love, that he laid down his life for us,
and we ought to lay down our lives for the brothers."
1 John 3:16

In the movie Shrek, towards the end of the movie, Shrek goes to Duloc to confess his love for princess Fiona. If you have seen the movie, you know that Fiona doesn't believe that Shrek was truly in love with her. Lord Farquaad made fun of Shrek for confessing his feelings for Fiona and said, " oh, this is precious! The ogre is in love with the princess!…." Shrek felt ashamed that he even told Fiona how he felt. But little did Shrek know that Fiona had a secret. She turned into an ogre every night. She went to the window as the sun set and transformed into an ogre. Lord Farquaad immediately ordered them both to be arrested, and Shrek was willing to risk his life to save Fiona.

Just like Shrek was willing to risk his life to save Fiona, all men can focus on ways that they can keep their wives or girlfriends safe with the gifts that God gave them. It doesn't matter if it's through physical, mental, emotional, or spiritual safety. We can protect them physically with the strength He gives us, and we can protect them by helping them through whatever they are going through mentally. We can also protect their spirituality by praying for them and with them every day. Hopefully, we will never have to lay down our lives for our wives or girlfriends, but if that ever does happen, we can remind ourselves how Jesus laid down His life for us.

1. Am I ever willing to give up my life for my wife or girlfriend?

____

____

____

____

____

2. How can I embrace giving up my life for my wife or girlfriend in the way God wants me to?

____

____

____

____

____

Dear God, please speak to my heart and help me realize how I can lay down my life, whether it's physically, spiritually, or mentally for my girlfriend or wife. Help me to give up my life for her to protect her spiritually, physically, mentally, and even emotionally. Thank you for helping me realize the best ways to be there for her in the same way that you are there for me. In Jesus' name, amen.

Day 29

Loving Your Enemies

*"But I say to you who hear, love your enemies,
do good to those who hate you."*
Luke 6:27

My sister has been fighting mental illness and alcoholism for over 30 years. When she drinks, she blames our family for things in her past that she can't let go of. She blames everyone in her life for everything that she has done wrong. I have tried to help her through her problems. I have prayed for her throughout her life and begged God to heal her physically, mentally, and spiritually. Whenever I tried to help her, she attacked me verbally and spiritually. I don't see her as my enemy, and I still love her, but it got to be too much for me with the mental and spiritual abuse she was putting me through. I had to sever all communication with her to protect myself and my family. I still love her and pray daily for God to save her, but it pains me to not have a relationship with her. I just pray that she finds peace through God.

Just like this man prays for his sister every day to find peace through a relationship with God, we, too, can pray for those who hurt and persecute us. Showing those people God's love is the greatest gift we can ever give them. Only through Him can we continually show those people unconditional love, even if it's just through praying for them.

1. Am I allowing myself to love the people I consider to be my enemies?

____

____

____

____

2. How can I love my enemies and do good to those who persecute me?

____

____

____

____

Dear God, please help me to love the people that hurt me in the same way that you love the people who hurt you and persecuted you. Thank you that I don't have to be around the people that hurt me in order to protect myself, but I can use the most powerful weapon, which is prayer. Thank you for always giving me the strength to do good to those who hurt me. In Jesus' name, amen.

Day 30

Love Our Wives as Christ Loves Us

"Husbands, love your wives, as Christ loved
the church and gave himself up for her."
Ephesians 5:25

I have learned throughout my life that I must continually love my wife the way God loves her. It isn't always easy because we are both sinners and fall short of God's mark. We also fall short of each other's expectations every day. The good news is that God doesn't expect either of us to be perfect because only Jesus Himself is perfect. All I have to do is try my best to love my wife and ask God to tell me how to love her differently daily. Some days she needs physical love, while on hard mental health days, she needs prayers, hugs, and reassurance that God and I think she is enough. I have to be willing to give myself up for her, whether it is mentally, physically, or emotionally at any time that she needs me.

Just like this man prays for wisdom to love his wife daily, we can do the same thing. We can ask how our wives are doing every day and ask God to help us see how we can love them by praying for and with them. There is much to be gained just by being present with our wives when they have difficult days. God will give us the ability to know what steps to take to be present with our wives daily.

1. Am I loving my wife the way God wants me to love her?

____

____

____

____

____

2. How can I love my wife the way God loves her?

____

____

____

____

____

Dear God, please help me to love my wife the way that you love her. Help me to love her as you love the church. Please teach me how to give myself up for my wife daily in the same way that you gave up your life for us on the cross. Thank you for giving me the ability to love her spiritually, mentally, physically, and emotionally. In Jesus' name, amen.

Day 31

Dreams Increasing

"For when dreams increase and words grow many, there is vanity; but God is the one you must fear."
Ecclesiastes' 5:7

Abraham wanted to have a child more than anything. He was more than 100 years old and decided to take matters into his own hands instead of trusting that God would give him a son. He slept with his wife Sarah's maidservant Hagar and got her pregnant just so he would have a child. Sooner than later, he learned that the bigger his dreams were, the more his thoughts led him in the wrong direction. Abraham knew he had made a mistake and should have left the dreams of his heart in God's hands and in God's control instead of trying to do things on his own.

All men have dreams and wishes in their hearts. But so often, we forget that God is the one who gives us those dreams. We want to go after our dreams with everything we have within us, but we forget that God needs to be at the front of our dreams. Without Him, we can't fulfill any dreams. But with our focus on Him, we can fulfill every one of our dreams. Just like Abraham, we can realize that our dreams will come to pass if we leave them in God's hands instead of trying to control them ourselves. Even though it is hard to surrender control over our dreams, when we let God have control over them, we will feel peace instead of pain.

1. Am I allowing myself to dream the dreams God put in my heart, or am I only dreaming for myself?

____

____

____

____

____

2. How can I cling to the dreams God put in my heart and follow them with His leadership?

____

____

____

____

____

Dear God, please fill my heart with your dreams. Please help me to see your dreams for me in my everyday life. Thank you for giving me dreams that I can only fulfill through you. Please help me to accomplish your dreams for my life. In Jesus' name, amen.

DAY 32
STAY FAITHFUL TO YOUR WIFE

*"But as he considered these things, behold, an angel of
the Lord appeared to him in a dream, saying, "Joseph,
son of David, do not fear to take Mary as your wife, for
that which is conceived in her is from the Holy Spirit."*
MATHEW 1:20

Joseph was engaged to be married to Mary. She got the news from the angel of the Lord that she would give birth to a son named Jesus and didn't even know how to tell Joseph. She thought he wouldn't believe her when she told him it was an immaculate conception. When she told him, he had in mind to divorce her quietly to save her from public humiliation. But in a dream, an angel of the Lord appeared to Joseph, telling him to not be afraid to take Mary home as his wife. The angel assured him that she had not cheated on him and conceived Jesus by the Holy Spirit. Joseph knew from that day that he had to take Mary home to be his wife.

We can do what Joseph did. When we doubt our wives, we can ask God what He wants us to do and ask Him the best course of action. We can be brave like Joseph, even though he doubted what Mary had told him. God may not appear to us as often as He did in the dream that Joseph had, but He wants us to stay true to our wives no matter what. If we think our wives may have cheated on us, we can ask God to show us whether it is true or not through the prompting of the Holy Spirit.

1. Am I staying faithful to my wife?

____

____

____

____

____

2. In what ways can I show my wife that I'll always be faithful to her?

____

____

____

____

____

Dear God, thank you for my wife. Thank you for blessing us with each other in the holy unity of marriage. Please help me to stay faithful to her in every way possible. Help me to be like Joseph and never give up on my marriage or my wife. Thank you for allowing me to always be there for my wife. In Jesus' name, amen.

Day 33
Trust God's Plan

"For I know the plans I have for you, declares the Lord, plans for welfare and not for evil, to give you a future and a hope."
JEREMIAH 29:11

Even in his darkest hour of being thrown into the lion's den, Daniel didn't stop believing in God or that he would be delivered from the lions. He might have been afraid, but he didn't let fear stop his faith. Who wouldn't have been afraid in the middle of a dark den of hungry lions? Daniel knew that he would be saved because of his faith in God. God had a wonderful plan for Daniel's life that included bringing the king to know Him as his Lord and Savior. When King Darius went to check on Daniel, he found that the lions hadn't hurt Daniel. King Darius then issued a decree saying that everyone in his kingdom had to worship the God of Israel.

Even in Daniel's darkest hour, he didn't give up his faith. All men can learn to assume some of the same courage as Daniel. Even though he was thrown into the lion's den for worshipping God, Daniel knew that God had a plan for his future to help bring others to Christ through his experience. We can believe that same thing. Whenever we go through difficulties, we believe that God has a great plan and purpose for our lives. Those include plans to prosper and give us hope and a great future.

1. Have I trusted in God's plan for my life?

2. How can I really believe He will work everything out for my good and give me hope and a future?

Dear God, please help me to believe that your plans are good for me. Thank you that you have a great plan for my life and that you will never fail me. Thank you for always being here for me and for giving me secure hope for my future. Please help me to live my life according to your plan and not my own. Please help me to lead others to know you. In Jesus' name, amen.

Day 34

Speak God's Word faithfully

"Let the prophet who has a dream tell the dream, but let
him who has my word speak my word faithfully..."
Jeremiah 23:28

Peter wasn't afraid to speak God's word even though he was ridiculed, criticized, and even put to death for knowing and loving Jesus. Throughout his life, he boldly spoke about the great things God had done in his life and miracles, not by his own hands but by the power of God within him. Peter went on speaking God's words faithfully until the day God called him home to be with Him forever. Peter was willing to meet people right where they were to share the Gospel of Jesus, no matter the cost.

God wants us to speak His word boldly and do it gladly without worrying about what could happen to us. There is nothing more important than spreading the word of God to anyone and everyone we know, even those we don't know. We can spread His word by praying for and with the people around us. We can also ask people if they have ever wanted a relationship with Jesus. If they say yes, we can invite them to accept Jesus as their Lord and Savior. We can be willing to meet people exactly where they are, no matter what they have going on in their lives. We, too, can be like Peter and assume the same spirit of determination to proclaim God's good news from the time we are born until the day He calls us home.

1. Am I speaking God's word faithfully?

____

____

____

____

____

2. How can I speak about God without fear of ridicule?

____

____

____

____

____

Dear God, please help me to speak about you faithfully throughout my life, every single day. Thank you for giving me the honor and privilege to talk to you and about you to my friends, family, and children. I want to leave a legacy of following you in my life. Thank you for putting your word into my heart daily and for allowing me to know you as my Lord and Savior. In Jesus' name, amen.

Day 35
Don't Be Silent

"And the Lord said to Paul one night in a vision, "Do not
be afraid, but go on speaking and do not be silent...."
Acts 18:9

Paul wasn't afraid to speak about Jesus in public. Even when imprisoned, he didn't dial down his preaching about God or his worship of God. In prison, he continued to shout and praise God, whom he knew would deliver him from all troubles and tribulations. He knew none of the sufferings he was going through could compare to the joy coming to him. He knew the pains he was experiencing were all for the right reasons. He was glorifying Jesus as his Lord and Savior, no matter what it cost him. He even gave up his life for his faith.

We can assume some of the courage that Paul had and boldly proclaim God's goodness in our lives. No matter who calls us weird or hates us for our faith, we can stand firm and proclaim His glory every day of our lives, whether it's in our family life, at work, with our friends, or even with people, we don't know. Even if people try to silence us for our faith, we don't have to be silent because it's our job to tell others about Jesus and what He can do for them. It's our job to tell others to give themselves up for God's glory and help others have a personal relationship with Him.

1. Am I being silent or loud about my faith the way Paul was?

____

____

____

____

2. How can I boldly proclaim my faith in God without fear, no matter the circumstance?

____

____

____

____

Dear God, please help me to not be silent about my faith in you, no matter what may happen to me. Please help me to be bold when telling others about my faith and what it means to me. Please help me to explain You in a way that is easy for people to understand. Let others see the hope and joy that you have given to me and claim your love and eternal peace for themselves. In Jesus' name, amen.

Day 36

Never Lean on Your Own Understanding

*"Trust in the Lord with all your heart, and do
not lean on your own understanding."*
Proverbs 3:5

David trusted God when Saul searched for him to try and kill him. Even though his men told him to go after Saul and kill him before he got killed by Saul, David cried out to God for protection and believed God would protect and deliver him. He knew he couldn't take down Saul on his own, so he relied on God's strength to escape from Saul safely. He learned how to lean on God for everything that he went through, and he got through many struggles that he couldn't have gotten through without God in his life.

We can help ourselves to trust in God and lean not on our own understanding. If David can be delivered multiple times from Saul and from his mistake of having Uriah killed in battle and then having an affair with Uriah's wife Bathsheba, imagine what He can do for us, our marriages, and our children. When we trust in God instead of leaving everything in our hands, everything will fall into place at the right time. There's nothing He can't or won't do for us.

1. Do I trust in the Lord with all my heart?

2. How can I learn to trust in Him every day?

Dear God, please help me to trust you more than I trust myself. Please help me to lean on you to get through my everyday life. Help me to remember that it's better to turn to you instead of relying on my own strength. Thank you for directing my path and for guiding me. Help me to trust in you with all of my heart at all times. In Jesus' name, amen.

Day 37

Not Afraid

"When I am afraid, I put my trust in you. In
God, whose word I praise, in God I trust; I shall
not be afraid. What can flesh do to me?"
Psalm 56:3-11

In Shrek, when the donkey and Shrek go to rescue Princess Fiona from the dragon and the tower, the donkey admits to Shrek that he is afraid of walking on a rickety bridge over a boiling lake of lava. But Shrek sarcastically reassures him that he is right there with him and that they will tackle walking over the bridge one little baby step at a time. He tells the donkey not to look down and just keep walking. When the donkey steps onto the wrong board, he looks down at the boiling lava and is terrified. He didn't want to continue walking on the bridge, but then Shrek started swinging the bridge back and forth to make the donkey move faster and get him off the bridge.

That is the same thing that God does for our families and us. Sometimes we are so afraid that we forget to trust in God because we think it can't get any worse in our lives. God often shakes us up, so we turn back to Him and remember that we don't have to be afraid because God is always with us. There is nothing that this world can do to us unless we react to it and allow it to hurt us or disrupt our lives. Just like how Shrek distracted the donkey, God often distracts us from our pain long enough for us to realize that He was the one who got us through it.

1. Have I put my trust in God whenever I'm afraid?

2. Do I fully believe that God will protect me from all harm?

Dear God, please help me to trust in you whenever I am afraid. Please protect my family and me every day and help me to believe that you are with me in every situation. Thank you for reminding me that this life can't get to me as long as I keep my trust in you. In Jesus' name, amen.

Day 38

Commit Your Ways to God

"Commit your way to the Lord; trust in him, and he will act."
Psalm 37:5

David firmly believed that God would deliver him from every trouble because he had seen God work in such mighty ways in his life. Even though he had made many mistakes, including having Uriah killed in battle and sleeping with his wife Bathsheba, he knew he could always turn to God at any time. Whenever David made a mistake, he came before God in reverent prayer, saying how sorry he was and repented. God acted on David's behalf in many ways, and David never missed an opportunity to praise God for what He did.

We, too, can come before God and ask Him to act on our behalf and on behalf of our families, marriage, children's lives, and work lives. Just like when we apologize for our mistakes before God in prayer, when we make mistakes in our marriage, we talk to our wives and ask them for forgiveness. When we make mistakes with our children, we approach them on their level, no matter how old they are, and let them know that we are sorry for hurting them. When we make mistakes in our jobs, we learn from them. We may not always get second chances with our families or work, but God gives us second chances. We know that as long as we commit our lives to the Lord, He will act on our behalf.

1. Have I committed my plans to the Lord?

____

____

____

____

____

2. Do I trust that He will act for me on my behalf?

____

____

____

____

____

Dear God, please help me to trust in you and believe that you will act for me on my behalf. Thank you for always working on my behalf. Even when I don't see how I will make it away out of situations, I know you will and always are working on my behalf, in Jesus' name, amen.

Day 39
Believe That We Receive It

"Therefore I tell you, whatever you ask in prayer, believe
that you have received it, and it will be yours."
Mark 11:24

Daniel firmly believed that God would save him no matter what he went through. Look at how he prayed in faith even when thrown into the lion's den. If he was any other person at any other time, he would have been eaten alive by the lions. But because of his faith in the face of severe adversity, God granted his request to deliver him from the mouths of the lions. Daniel believed that he would be saved by God and didn't doubt what he prayed for. He firmly believed that God would save him, and his faith saw him through one of the toughest times of his life.

We can be like Daniel and believe that whatever we ask for in prayer will be granted to us if it is His will. If our prayers align with God's will, He will grant them for our sake. When we pray for our marriage to improve with God's help, He will grant it as long as our eyes are set on Him. He will grant it when we pray for our kids to succeed in school, high school, or college. If He wants us to get a promotion at work and we believe that we will receive it, He will allow us to get the promotion. We can pray for anything and believe that we will receive it.

1. Do I firmly believe that whatever I ask for in prayer, I'll receive it, or do I doubt it?

____

____

____

____

____

2. How can I change my doubt into believing that God will grant me whatever I ask for in prayer?

____

____

____

____

____

Dear God, please help me to believe that I can and will receive whatever I ask for in prayer. Please help me to believe and pray like I already received what I asked for every day of my life. In Jesus' name, amen.

Day 40

We Know God's Name

"And those who know your name put their trust in you, for you, O Lord, have not forsaken those who seek you."
Psalm 9:10

Abraham might have looked dumb to people who didn't understand that he was given directions by God to build the ark. But Abraham trusted God and His plan for his life. Many didn't understand why he was building the ark. Every time he explained why he was building it, he looked like he was crazy until the flood happened. He warned people that the flood was coming way before it actually occurred. He even got two of every animal and put them in the ark. Then he gathered up his family and got all of them in the ark before the flood happened. When the flood happened, everyone who wasn't on the ark perished.

We can trust God no matter what goes on in our lives. As long as we seek Him in everything we do, He will not forsake us. We have a personal relationship with Him. We can help people in our lives come to know that the promises in God's word are true. Whenever someone doesn't understand why we are working for the Lord, it gives us the opportunity and privilege to share Jesus with them. They may or may not believe us when we tell them how good God is, but we know He will never forsake the people we talk to about Him or us. We know that we are doing the right thing by trying to point others to the free gift of salvation in Jesus Christ as their Savior.

1. Have I sought after God in my everyday life?

____

____

____

____

____

2. In what ways can I put my trust in God every day?

____

____

____

____

____

Dear God, please help me to put my trust in you and to seek you in everything I do. Thank you for not forsaking me and for always guiding me down the right path. Thank you for sending the beautiful rainbow at the end of the flood, which symbolized that you would never flood the earth again. In Jesus' name, amen.

DAY 41
RENEW YOUR MIND

"Do not be conformed to this world, but be
transformed by the renewal of your mind, that by
testing you may discern what is the will of God,
what is good and acceptable and perfect."
ROMANS 12:2

Saul gave in to the patterns of sin in this world, especially in his heart, when he persecuted and killed Christians just for following Christ. But on the way to Damascus, Jesus allowed him to be transformed by the complete and utter renewal of his mind. No one would have believed that Saul was transformed into Paul if they didn't see it. Saul was transformed into Paul by Jesus' power. He wanted Paul to make a difference in people's lives for the good of the Gospel. God knew how to transform Saul into Paul and make his life good, acceptable, and perfect. Saul went from killing Christians to Paul, who went to the ends of the earth just to share the good news of the Gospel, no matter what it cost him.

We can allow ourselves to be renewed and transformed by the renewal of our minds every day. We can ask God to show us what His will is and what is good, acceptable, and perfect. He will get us through anything and help us to know which paths to take in every area of our lives. Just like he transformed Saul into Paul, we can allow ourselves to be transformed in God's way. After all, His ways are better than ours.

1. Am I able to discern God's will for my life?

____

____

____

____

____

2. How am I being tested, and what can I do to make it through each test?

____

____

____

____

____

Dear God, please help me to persevere
through any tests that come my way, whether
it's a test in my marriage, with my children,
at work, or with my friends. Please help me
to know that through you, I can persevere
through anything. In Jesus' name, amen.

Day 42

Stand Firm in Faith

"Be watchful, stand firm in the faith, act like men,
be strong. Let all that you do be done in love."
1 Corinthians 16:13-14

Abraham stood firm in faith when told he would have Isaac in his old age. He didn't lose faith when told he would become many nations' father. He also didn't lose his faith when he was told by God to sacrifice his son Isaac as a sacrifice to God. He was watchful, stood firm in his faith, and stood strong. He learned to let everything he did be done in love. He loved his son with all his heart and trusted God enough that he was willing to sacrifice Isaac. But God saw that he was about to sacrifice Isaac and sent a ram for Abraham to sacrifice instead.

We can be strong and let everything we do be done in love. Whether it is picking our kids up at school or being there for their sports practice or games, or just being there for our kids whenever they need us. We can also be strong for our wives during hard times. We can pray for and with them and our kids. Making prayer a habit with our families can only help strengthen our relationship with our families and with God.

1. Is all that I'm doing being done in love?

____

____

____

____

2. In what ways can I be strong for my family in my faith?

____

____

____

____

Dear God, please help me to stand firm in my faith. Help me to do and say everything with love in my heart. Help me to remain watchful in my faith every day. Please help me to follow you into any uncharted territory with full faith that you will help me make the right decisions just like Abraham did. In Jesus' name, amen.

DAY 43

MIGHTY IN BATTLE

*"Who is this King of glory? The Lord, strong
and mighty, the Lord, mighty in battle!"*
PSALM 24:8

The Lord is strong in any battle we face. He is also the king of glory, and He is stronger than any of us ever could be. When we think we can't go on, that is when God tells us through the Holy Spirit to continue to try our best in everything we do. David knew that God was the king of glory and that He would forever be. Despite his battle, David knew that God would deliver him from all of it. He declared in this psalm and many other psalms that he knew God was on his side. He knew God was a mighty warrior fighting alongside him.

We can have the faith and confidence that David had in God. He is strong and able to help us through everything we face. We can go through our daily lives confidently, saying, "There is nothing God won't do for me." "With God, I will succeed in my marriage, with my relationship with my kids, and at work. I can do everything through Christ who strengthens me." "I am confident and strong with God's power within me." "I'm a confident warrior who will succeed with God's help."

1. How has God enabled me to be a warrior for my faith?

____

____

____

____

____

2. In what ways can I encourage others to be a warrior for their faith?

____

____

____

____

____

Dear God, please help me to be a warrior for my faith. Help me to bring others to know you through my words and actions. Thank you for allowing me to know that you always fight my battles for me and with me. In Jesus' name, amen.

DAY 44
NOT THE END

"And you will hear of wars and rumors of
wars. See that you are not alarmed, for this
must take place, but the end is not yet."
MATHEW 24:6

Even though there were, are, and will be difficult times ahead, this verse tells us that even though there will be troubles, we don't have to be alarmed by the things happening in the world. The end is not near. There will be rumors of wars, but they will be nothing compared to the joy that awaits us in eternity in heaven. Even though many men in the Bible were hated because of their strong faith in God, they didn't turn their back on God because they knew He was with them.

The end is not happening yet; even when it happens, God will be with us just like He promised to be with us all of our lives until we go to heaven. There might be wars and rumors, but we don't have to be alarmed. Because God is always with us. He warned us that these times would come upon us. But He also promised us that He would always be with us. He promised that He would always help us through difficult times. Even though we will have people hate us because of our faith, we should never turn our back on God because He never turns His back on us.

1. Am I alarmed by what is happening in my life?

____

____

____

____

____

2. What steps can I take to correct the things that are within my control?

____

____

____

____

____

Dear God, please help me to not be alarmed by the things that are happening around me. Please help me to trust in you at all times and to know that even at the end of my life, I have a great victory waiting for me in heaven. In Jesus' name, amen.

Day 45

Look at Blessings

"For we do not wrestle against flesh and blood, but against the rulers, against the authorities, against the cosmic powers over this present darkness, against the spiritual forces of evil in the heavenly places."
EPHESIANS 6:12

Even though Job went through so much turmoil in his life, he never gave up his faith in God. He never turned away from God. Even though he knew he was wrestling with the spiritual forces of evil in the heavenly realm, he never once turned away from God. If anything, the troubles he faced only drew him closer to God. God never abandoned him in any way, shape, or form.

This world has more blessings than curses because of God's love for us. We can look for the blessings in our everyday life instead of looking at the struggles of our everyday life. There is nothing we can't get through. We can rest assured that we not only wrestle against the pressures of the flesh every day, but we wrestle against the darkness of this world. Even though we wrestle against those things daily, God is with us in every situation. We will know that God got us through them when we get through to the other side of our struggles.

1. How am I wrestling against flesh and blood and against the darkness of this world every day?

____

____

____

____

____

2. How can I resist the evil of this world and cling to God for mental and physical safety?

____

____

____

____

____

Dear God, thank you for protecting me mentally, physically, spiritually, and emotionally every day. Thank you for always being here for me. Please help me to resist evil and cling to your truths every day. In Jesus' name, amen.

Day 46

Honor Your Marriage

"Marriage should be honored by all, and the
marriage bed kept pure, for God will judge the
adulterer and all the sexually immoral."
Hebrews 13:4

Many men in the Bible didn't keep marriage sacred as God commanded them to. These included David, Abraham, Solomon, King Saul, and many others. They knew they'd made horrible mistakes by being unfaithful to their wives. Still, they repented and apologized for their mistakes. They suffered a lot for their mistakes, but they also became stronger. David knelt before God and begged for forgiveness. Abraham repented and asked God for forgiveness for sleeping with Hagar to have a child. Solomon knew he'd slept with too many women and repented for his sins.

Just like those men, we are supposed to put our marriage as our top priority. We are not to commit adultery because adultery is a serious sin. But God can help us know how we should treat our spouse every day, even if it is sometimes hard to love or even like them. God will always give us the right things to do and say to our spouses. He will help us remain faithful to our wives.

1. How am I honoring my marriage every day?

____

____

____

____

____

2. In what ways can I honor my wife and my marriage every day?

____

____

____

____

____

Dear God, thank you for the sanctity of marriage and that it is designed by you for the blessing and goodness of all mankind. You even said in Genesis that it wasn't good for man to be alone, so you gave him a helper. Help me to honor my wife and keep our marriage pure in every way. Help me to honor our marriage in the way you want it to be honored. In Jesus' name, amen.

DAY 47

THERE'S NO TEMPTATION YOU CAN'T BEAR

"No temptation has overtaken you except what is common to mankind. And God is faithful; he will not let you be tempted beyond what you can bear. But when you are tempted, he will also provide a way out so that you can endure it."
1 CORINTHIANS 10:13

Jesus was tempted three times in the wilderness, but He had the ultimate weapon. He was God's one and only Son and knew how to fight temptation with scripture. When tempted to turn stones into bread, He said, "man does not live by bread alone." When He was tempted to throw Himself off the highest building in the town, He said, "it is written do not put the Lord your God to the test." Tempted to worship the wrong guy, He said, "it is written worship the Lord your God and serve Him only."

Just like Jesus resisted temptation, we can resist it and stand firm against it. There is no temptation that we aren't given way out of. Look at what Jesus was able to do. He got out of temptation through reciting scripture. He gives us the same power of God and the Holy Spirit daily. There is no temptation that we can't get through with His help. He gives us ways to withstand and overcome every temptation.

1. How am I tempted?

____

____

____

____

____

2. What other scriptures can I say daily to resist temptation?

____

____

____

____

____

Dear God, please help me to resist temptation every day. Thank you for giving me a way out of every temptation, no matter what I face daily. Help me to turn to you and to even recite scripture whenever I feel temptation lurking in my mind, heart, or body. Thank you for giving me the strength to resist it. In Jesus' name, amen.

Day 48

Eternal Life

"For God so loved the world, that he gave
his only Son, that whoever believes in him
should not perish but have eternal life."

John 3:16

God loves us so much that He knew He had to figure out a way to bring all people to salvation. He gave up His one and only Son and allowed Him to come to earth to save everyone from sin and death. He loved us so much that He was willing to sacrifice His only Son for the entire world's salvation. He wants everyone to come to know Him and for us to help others be saved. He can and will change lives if people give Him a chance. He knew that some people would not accept His message of hope and love, but those that do accept Him will have eternal life in heaven.

We can teach our children, wives, and friends about the benefit of having a relationship with God and making Him a priority in our lives. We can pray for and with our wives every day before we go to work. We can say simple prayers like: "Lord, please help us stay close to you and to know you personally. Help our marriage to thrive with you in the center of it." If our children ask us about God, we can come down to their level and explain how God can and will change their lives through daily scripture reading, prayer, and just talking to God about their daily lives. Whenever we have struggles at work, we can ask God how to handle them professionally.

1. Have people been willing to listen to what I tell them about the goodness of God?

2. What can I do when someone rejects my news about Jesus?

Dear God, please help me to not get discouraged when someone doesn't want to hear about Jesus. Please help me to tell others about the goodness of life through knowing you as my Lord and Savior. Thank you for always giving me the courage to tell others about you. In Jesus' name, amen.

Day 49
Shake the Dust Off Your Feet

"If anyone will not welcome you or listen to your words, leave that home or town and shake the dust off your feet. Truly I tell you; it will be more bearable for Sodom and Gomorrah on the day of judgment than for that town."
Mathew 10:14-15

When men in the Bible preached God's word, like Peter, Paul, and John, they didn't let the rejection of other people stop them. They didn't let anything stop them from telling the world the good news about God. Jesus didn't let anything stop Him from telling the world His good news. He even gave up His life for everyone on the cross in the most painful manner imaginable. If anyone didn't listen to what Paul, Peter, John, or Jesus was saying, they all just got up, dusted off their feet, and moved on to the next town to talk to the people there. Even if people didn't accept what was coming out of their mouths, they still did what God was calling them to do.

We can summon the courage that Peter, John, Paul, and Jesus had whenever we go to different towns in our state, across the country, or even out of the country to spread the Gospel. We can go everywhere God tells us to go with our families, work friends, or just by ourselves to spread the good news of Jesus. Whenever we go to a different city, and people don't want to listen to us, we can remember that when people don't accept what we say, we can leave that town or home and try spreading the gospel in another city or town and see if anyone will listen to the message of the gospel there.

1. Am I trying hard enough to spread the gospel, or do I need to do more?

____

____

____

____

____

2. When someone doesn't accept Jesus, how can God help me walk away knowing I tried my best?

____

____

____

____

____

Dear God, please help me to spread the Gospel to everyone I meet. Please help me to remember what you said if someone doesn't listen to me, to dust off my feet and move on to the next town. Even when someone doesn't accept my message, please help me to remember that I am doing the work for you. Thank you for always allowing me to know that even if people don't accept the things I say about you, that I am doing the right thing by being a witness for you. In Jesus' name, amen.

Day 50
Work with All Your Heart

"Whatever you do, work at it with all your heart,
as working for the Lord, not for human masters."
Colossians 3:23

In the movie Die Hard, John McClane worked with all his heart to rescue his wife, Holly, and the other hostages from the Naka Tomi Plaza crisis. He did everything he could to rescue the hostages and to prove to Holly that he still loved her. If you've seen Die Hard, there is a scene in the middle of the movie where John McClane is talking to Al Powell, and he says, "I want you to find my wife… tell her that she's the best thing that ever happened to a guy like me…. She's heard me say, "I love you" a thousand times. But she never heard me say I'm sorry. I want you to tell her that John says he's sorry." John wanted his wife to know how much she meant to him, especially if he didn't survive. He worked at saving his wife and the other hostages with all of his heart and took great risks.

We can take great risks and work at everything as if we are working for the Lord. We should stay focused on the Lord in our personal and work lives, especially in our marriages. Our marriages are gifts from God and should be treated as an honor and privilege. We can remind ourselves to work for the Lord and not for our own human desires. When we work for the Lord, our plans will succeed.

1. Am I working for God with all my heart?

2. What steps can I take to work for God with all my heart?

Dear God, please help me to do everything as if I'm doing it for you. Help me to work for you and not to satisfy my own human desires. Thank you for giving me the ability to reach out to people on a deeply personal level. Thank you for helping me to work for you in every area of my life, whether it is in my personal life, work life, or with my friends. In Jesus' name, amen.

Day 51

Make Known the Paths of Life

"You make known to me the path of life; in
your presence there is fullness of joy; at your
right hand are pleasures forevermore."
Psalm 16:11

David was a man who loved to talk to God in any situation, anywhere, and everywhere he went. Whether he was fighting for his life, worried about his health, depressed, or on his knees praising God for His faithfulness, David always talked to God. God made known to him the path of life. God didn't look the other way when he had Uriah killed in battle and slept with his wife. Because of his adultery, David lost his son. But David had victories in his life. He won battles and defeated Goliath, the giant. He knew that God would continue to show him the paths that he should take and reward him with the pleasures of eternity.

Just like David, we can talk to God anytime, anywhere, no matter where we are. We can have the same confidence that he had in God. He will make known the paths of each of our lives as long as we focus on Him. Every day we can be diligent in prayer and ask Him to show us exactly where to go in life. We can guide our wives and kids to seek God's plans for their lives. We can reassure them that as long as they stick with Him, He will show them the right paths just like He does for us. We can be fully immersed in joy in His presence whenever we need a boost in our spirits.

1. Do I firmly believe that God will show me His paths for my life and fill my life with pleasure?

2. What steps can I take to see the fullness of joy in God's presence?

Dear God, please help me to find and pursue your paths in my life every day. Thank you that I can come into your presence at any time, no matter where I am. Thank you for letting me have a pleasure-filled life according to your grace and mercy. Help me to show others around me the pleasures of having a relationship with you. In Jesus' name, amen.

Day 52
Christ Lives in You

"I have been crucified with Christ. It is no longer
I who live, but Christ who lives in me. And the life
I now live in the flesh I live by faith in the Son of
God, who loved me and gave himself for me."
Galatians 2:20

Paul knew that he had been crucified with Christ and that Christ lived within him. The old version of him as Saul was completely gone. The Christians he used to kill and persecute, he actually started telling them about Jesus. Jesus radically changed his life and helped him live for God in a way he never had. Paul eventually ended up giving up his life for his faith, just like Jesus did.

Christ lives in each one of us. We can help everyone we meet to come to know that the hope of glory is in us at all times. As the male figures in our families' lives, it is important to help them know that Christ lives in them. It's important to remember that even though we all live in the flesh, we can teach our families to live with the love of Christ no matter where they may be or who they are interacting with. We don't just live for ourselves, but we live for God daily. We have the honor and privilege to bring others to Christ. Even though we may be afraid to talk to others about God, we can assume the courage that Paul had. When it says we have been crucified with Christ, it means that the old version of ourselves is gone, and a new version of ourselves is being born daily when we keep God first.

1. How can I believe that Christ lives in me every day?

____

____

____

____

____

2. What steps can I take to live my life by faith?

____

____

____

____

____

Dear God, please help me to live my life by faith every day. Thank you that I don't live on my own anymore and that you are always with me and within me. I might live in the flesh, but I know through you I can live by faith. In Jesus' name, amen.

DAY 53
TESTING WITH PLEASURE

"I said in my heart, "Come now, I will test you with pleasure;
enjoy yourself." But behold, this also was vanity."
ECCLESIASTES 2:12

King Solomon went after several different women. He had more than 700 concubines. He eventually realized that what he was chasing after was completely meaningless. He thought he deserved to party, eat, drink and be merry every chance. But he was given a strong dose of reality and figured out that everything he wanted was meaningless. He tested himself with earthly pleasures just like we all tend to do. But after a while, Solomon chased after Jesus.

God wants us to enjoy ourselves and not stress over the little things in life. But this verse warns us not to go chasing after what is meaningless in our lives. That means not going after other women when we are married to our wives and not abandoning our families when things get difficult. It means not throwing the towel on our marriage when we argue with our wives. It also heads a warning to not chase after other meaningless things. Pleasures in this world are meaningless compared to the glory of heaven. We are tested with pleasure every day. God gives us the free will to choose whether or not we give into meaningless pleasures of drugs, alcohol, or partying. We can resist temptation and enjoy earthly pleasures in moderation. It doesn't mean we can't enjoy the friends, family, or work opportunities that He puts in our lives. Still, He wants us to learn to enjoy the little things instead of indulging in everything we want.

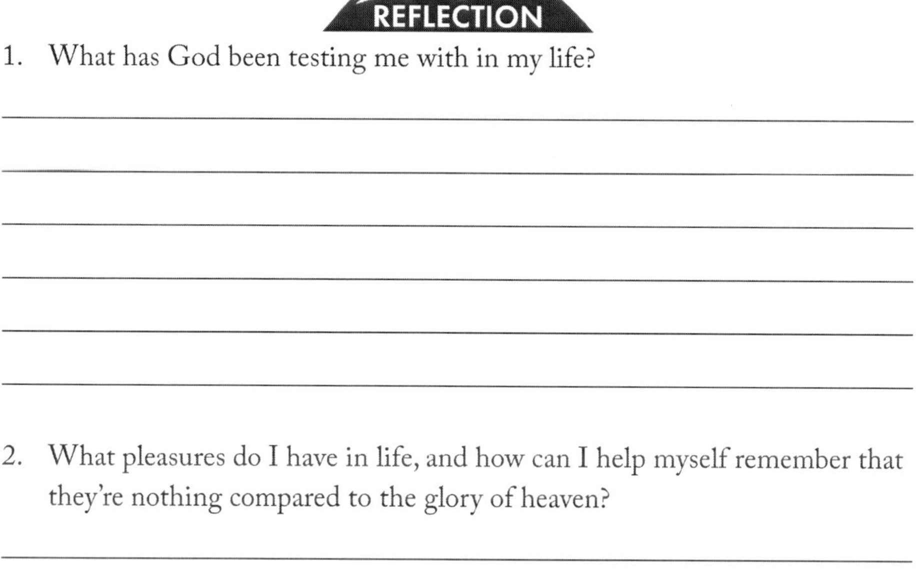

1. What has God been testing me with in my life?

____

____

____

____

____

____

2. What pleasures do I have in life, and how can I help myself remember that they're nothing compared to the glory of heaven?

____

____

____

____

____

____

Dear God, please help me not to forget that any of the pleasures that I have aren't of my own doing. They are from you and only you. Please test me to live my life for you and only you. Whenever I go astray, please lead me in the right direction. Help me to remember that every pleasure on earth is vanity compared to the glories I'll see in heaven. In Jesus' name, amen.

Day 54

The Lord Takes Pleasure in You

"For the Lord takes pleasure in his people;
he adorns the humble with salvation."
PSALM 149:4

The Lord took pleasure in Jesus so much that He sent Him to die for everyone's sins. Peter loved Jesus so much that he jumped out of the boat to walk toward Jesus on the water. John the Baptist was the one who prepared the way for the Lord and baptized people in Jesus' name. Daniel didn't deny his faith when he was faced with the lions. Shadrach, Meshach, and Abednego refused to worship any other God except the God of Israel. Abraham obeyed what God called him to do, and God honored him by making him the father of many nations. God adorned every one of those humble men with salvation.

The Lord takes the same pleasure in all of us and adorns us with salvation every time we act in humble manners. Whether we open the door for our spouse or someone who is a complete stranger at the store, He loves it when we go out of our way to help others. He loves it when we willingly give our time to help out in our community. He loves when we give up our precious time listening to our wives, children, and friends when they are going through hard times. God smiles when we listen to people who need help and offer to pray for and with them instead of judging them. When we stand up for our faith instead of renouncing our faith in the face of danger, God smiles on us.

1. How do I let myself believe that God loves me and takes pleasure in me?

2. What can I do to help others believe how loved they are by God?

Dear God, please help me to remember that I'm loved by you in ways that I can't even fathom. Please help me to believe that you actually take pleasure in me even though I make mistakes. Help me to remind people in my life that you take pleasure in them and delight in them. Thank you for taking pleasure in me no matter what. In Jesus' name, amen.

Day 55

He Keeps His Promises

"The Lord is not slow to fulfill his promise as some count slowness, but is patient toward you, not wishing that any should perish, but that all should reach repentance."
2 Peter 3:9

God is not slow in keeping His promises. In His promises, we find pleasure. Those pleasures of knowing God can never be taken away from us because once we have a relationship with God, nothing else matters. We are secured in our salvation and in God's everlasting love. Look at the pleasures He brought Abraham after the flood- He gave them a sure sign of his promises by showing them the rainbow, which was and still is a sure sign that He would never flood the earth again. Look at the salvation He gave us through Jesus dying on the cross. That salvation is the most important pleasure that we can ever have. David knew he would have victory over the giant Goliath before even fighting him through God.

Just because we don't always see the pleasures of this life in the ways we expect ourselves to doesn't mean we won't ever see them. The simple fact is that God keeps His promises. We can take in His promises when we get married. We promise to love, honor, and cherish our wives. We can be there for them through good and bad times from life until death. God gives us the simple pleasures of living a happy life with our spouse. Other simple pleasures in this life include listening to our children laughing with their friends and spending quality time with our grandchildren.

1. How can I help others know that God keeps Hus promises every day, even when I don't see them?

____

____

____

____

____

2. In what ways can I help others reach repentance?

____

____

____

____

____

Dear God, please help me to reach others with your goodness. Help me to tell others that you don't want anyone to perish. Thank you that you are not slow in keeping your promises, even when I don't see things happening. Help me to trust in your timing and not my own. In Jesus' name, amen.

DAY 56
SHOW HONOR TO EVERYONE

"Let love be genuine. Abhor what is evil; hold fast to what is good. Love one another with brotherly affection. Outdo one another in showing honor. Do not be slothful in zeal, be fervent in spirit, serve the Lord. Rejoice in hope, be patient in tribulation, be constant in prayer."
ROMANS 12:9

Jesus is the only one who loved everyone on earth genuinely enough. He loved the people who ridiculed and criticized Him. He loved the people who tried to trick Him into saying and doing the wrong things on the Sabbath-the Pharisees. He forgave Peter when he told Jesus that He would never die on the cross. He also forgave the people who didn't believe in Him, spit on Him, mocked Him, and nailed Him to the cross to die on Good Friday. Jesus abhorred what was evil and outdid everyone by doing good to people. He loved His disciples with true brotherly affection and was not slow in zeal or spirit. He served His heavenly Father faithfully. In the garden, He was reverent in prayer and patient with His disciples when they couldn't keep watch with Him for one hour.

We can be like Jesus and be genuine with our families. We can teach our children what it's like to do good to those around us and serve people faithfully. We can show honor to people even if they don't honor us. We can also be happy and content in our jobs no matter what happens. We can teach our children to serve the Lord faithfully and to never give up during hard times. We can also teach them how to forgive and pray as Jesus did.

1. How can I be consistent in prayer and hold fast to what is good?

____

____

____

____

____

2. In what ways can I show honor to people in my life?

____

____

____

____

____

Dear God, please help me to show honor to the people I interact with. Please help me to stay consistent in prayer and to serve you faithfully. Help me to show brotherly affection. Thank you for giving me the ability to be patient in times of affliction. In Jesus' name, amen.

Day 57
Honor Your Parents

"Honor your father and your mother, as the Lord your God commanded you, that your days may be long, and that it may go well with you in the land that the Lord your God is giving you."
Deuteronomy 5:16

Joseph honored his father and mother, Jacob and Rachel, by studying what Jacob wanted and doing what they asked him to do. One day Jacob asked Joseph to go where his brothers had their sheep grazing. If you've read the story, you know that Joseph's brothers were jealous of him for being Jacob's favorite son. They plotted to kill him but instead decided to sell him into slavery. The brothers dishonored their mother and father by selling Joseph into slavery.

Honoring parents takes a lot of work, especially as men transition into adulthood and parenthood. We can learn how to model our parents' behavior in a Godly way and raise our children in the love of the Lord. If we have grandchildren one day, we can teach them about Jesus and His love for them. We can consider and teach ourselves, our children, and grandchildren how important it is to honor our parents even if they annoy or anger us. Even when we disagree with them, we should still honor them so that we may have a long life.

1. How am I honoring my father and mother?

____

____

____

____

____

2. In what ways can I honor my mother and father even more than I do now?

____

____

____

____

____

____

Dear God, please help me to learn how to honor my mother and father even more than I do now. Thank you for my mother and father and for blessing me with a family that loves me. Help me to honor them in the way that you love and honor them. In Jesus' name, amen.

Day 58
Suffering Unjustly

"Honor everyone. Love the brotherhood. Fear God. Honor the emperor. Servants, be subject to your masters with all respect, not only to the good and gentle but also to the unjust. For this is a gracious thing, when, mindful of God, one endures sorrows while suffering unjustly."
1 Peter 2:17-19

The Marines have a very close brotherhood with their brothers in arms. They would willingly give up their lives for one another without a second thought. They honor their brothers, both alive and deceased, with military send-offs and welcome-home honors. They are taught to not only honor and respect the people they're fighting alongside but they are taught to respect the authority of their sergeants and commanding officers. They're also taught to be servants to those who are in need. The men in the Marines can see heavy combat, and it changes them in ways we will never fully know. They endure sorrows that not many people know about. They suffer unjust things like missing their families, losing a limb, or dying just to protect our country.

With God's help, we can assume some of that courage that the Marines have in our faith walk. We can gladly serve those who we may not like. We can honor and respect the authority figures in our lives, whether they are our families, friends, cops, or especially God. We can be respectful of all people, no matter if they are nice or evil toward us. Following Jesus is no easy task, but we can make ourselves ready for the challenge every day by praying and spending time in His word.

1. How have I loved the friends God has placed in my life with the brotherly love of Christ?

____

____

____

____

____

2. In what ways can I be good to those who are unjust to me?

____

____

____

____

____

Dear God, please help me to honor everyone in my life with love. Help me to be nice to those who have authority over me and to do good to those who are unjust to me. Thank you for allowing me to be mindful of you whenever I suffer injustice for proclaiming your great name. In Jesus' name, amen.

Day 59

Showing Honor

"Love one another with brotherly affection.
Outdo one another in showing honor."
Romans 12:10

Job honored God and never went against Him, even when his life was so close to being taken away from him. His family wanted him to renounce his faith, but he absolutely refused. Whatever he said, drank, or ate was all in honor of the Lord. He was the most honorable man in the Bible. He never turned away from God no matter what went on.

We can learn a thing or two as to how we can honor God, our families, our spouses, our children, and anyone else we come in contact with. Whatever we do, we should do it all for the glory of God. Whatever we eat or drink, we should do it in moderation and for the glory of God. When we eat sweets or drink alcohol, we should enjoy it all in moderation and not excess. When we eat anything, we shouldn't gorge, or binge eat. Even though glorifying God in everything we say and do can be hard, we can just do our best. That is all He wants us to do.

1. Am I honoring God in all I say and do?

____

____

____

____

____

2. In what ways can I honor God even more, every day?

____

____

____

____

____

Dear God, thank you for allowing me the privilege to honor you in everything I say and do on a daily basis. Help me to honor you in the thoughts I think and with what I put into and on my body. Keep my thoughts pure and holy. In Jesus' name, amen.

Day 60

Take No Honor for Yourself

"And no one takes this honor for himself, but only when called by God, just as Aaron was."
Hebrews 5:4

Aaron had a humble heart when he finally realized what Moses was trying to do: freeing the Israelites from slavery. At first, Aaron didn't like that Moses had come back, but he warmed up to him. Aaron eventually realized that he was called by God to help Moses out. He even made the bold move to walk into the Red Sea before everyone else, and he let his pride go and helped Moses lead the Israelites to freedom. But he also knew he couldn't take all the credit because it was Moses' assignment from God.

Sometimes, we, as men, think we can do everything for ourselves and for other people. But we must remember that we can never do anything without God's help. We can do things we never even thought possible with God's help. We don't need to take the honor of accomplishing things at work or when we do things for our spouses. We don't need to be recognized for making them dinner after a hard day or putting the dishes away just to be thanked. We can instead have a humble heart when we do something inspiring or nice. We are called by God to be servants to other people.

REFLECTION

1. Do I firmly believe that I'm called by God just like Aaron was?

2. In what ways can I humble myself under God's will?

PRAYER

Dear God, please help me to be humble towards you and to work for you every day of my life just as Moses and Aaron did. Please help me to never take any honor for myself but to give you the glory you deserve instead. In Jesus' name, amen.

Day 61

Sanctified Through Christ

"May God himself, the God of peace, sanctify you through and through. May your whole spirit, soul and body be kept blameless at the coming of our Lord Jesus Christ."
1 Thessalonians 5:23

Paul wanted everyone to come to know Jesus as their Lord and Savior. Even when he was imprisoned for preaching the Gospel, he knew that the peace of God would sustain him in every situation. Even though he would be punished for preaching the Gospel, he knew that his body, spirit, and soul would be kept blameless. When he accepted Jesus as his Lord and Savior, he had a complete transformation in his mind, body, and soul. He encouraged everyone he came in contact with to live blameless lives as much as possible. Even though they would sin, he wanted everyone to be sanctified and know Jesus.

God is the God of all peace and never wants us to be at war within ourselves. But unfortunately, there are times when we are at war within ourselves. During those times, we start doubting our abilities. But God wants His peace to flood our minds, hearts, and souls no matter what we go through. With God's help, we can be kept blameless in our bodies, minds, and souls. We don't have to surrender to the war that might be raging inside us. Instead, we can stand firm in our faith and know that God will help us through all difficult times. There is nothing He won't get us through.

1. How can I repent and be blameless before the coming of the Lord?

____

____

____

____

____

2. What can I do to help other men have peace in their lives through a relationship with God?

____

____

____

____

____

Dear God, please help me to repent of my sins and live a life that glorifies you every day. Help me to have peace throughout my life and to help others know what your true peace feels like. In Jesus' name, amen.

Day 62

The Attitude of Our Heart

"For the word of God is alive and active. Sharper than any double-edged sword, it penetrates even to dividing soul and spirit, joints and marrow; it judges the thoughts and attitudes of the heart."
HEBREWS 4:12

The Word of God is alive and active. Nothing can stop it from impacting those who believe it and receive it into their hearts. As men, Paul encourages us to think about how God's word is sharper than any double-edged sword. That means we must be aware of the power of our words when we tell people about God. We have to wait for just the right moment for the right words from God Himself to come out of our hearts and out of our mouths. It penetrates into anyone's heart that has received God and can also affect those who don't know God but want to know Him. He already knows every man's heart and soul and knows the thoughts every man feels in his heart.

We can be witnesses to every person and help them know the word of God just like Paul did. We can let people know that the word of God is alive and active in each of their lives, whether they realize it or not. God wants us to tell people that His word can divide hearts and souls from what people thought they once knew and wanted for their lives versus what they will have when they let God into their lives.

1. How can I change my attitude and heart around to make it purer and know God more?

2. In what ways can I help other people around me know that God's word is alive and active?

Dear God, please help me to focus on your word every day. Help me to help others know that your word is alive and active in our everyday lives. Thank you for helping my thoughts and actions become more like Yours. In Jesus' name, amen.

Day 63
You're God's Temple

"Do you not know that your bodies are temples of
the Holy Spirit, who is in you, whom you have
received from God? You are not your own;."
1 Corinthians 6:19

I work out every day, and it helps me feel good physically, mentally, and emotionally. I've been working out since I was young, but I didn't always work out safely in the way I should have. I pushed myself past the limits of what I probably should have. It wasn't until I was in my thirties that I accepted Jesus as my Lord and Savior, and I learned that my body is a temple. Once I heard that my body was a temple, I started to eat better and work out more safely. I even told my daughter that her body is a temple and to be honored by God, whether she is eating and drinking, driving, working out, or anything else.

Everyone forgets that our bodies aren't our own and that they are on loan for us to use until we get called to heaven. Just like this man didn't know that his body was a temple until he was in his thirties, every man can learn how to treat his body with respect it deserves. That means no matter what we are doing, whatever we eat or drink, we should honor our bodies because they are given to us by God, and we should use them for His glory.

1. How can I treat my body as a temple from God every day?

____

____

____

____

2. How can I remind myself that the Holy Spirit is in my body and that my body is a temple?

____

____

____

____

Dear God, thank you for reminding me that my body is a temple from you. Please help me to treat it as one every day. Thank you for the reminder that I am not my own and that my body is only on loan from you. Help me to honor my body. In Jesus' name, amen.

Day 64

Gain the World or Lose Your Soul

"For what will it profit a man if he gains the
whole world and forfeits his soul? Or what
shall a man give in return for his soul?"
Mathew 16:26

In TobyMac's song "Lose My Soul," the Christian singer sings about how he didn't want to gain the whole world and lose his soul if he didn't stay focused on God. The lyrics even say, "since I got the call, no more Saul, now I'm Paul." He talks about how it doesn't help anyone to lose their soul yet gain the world. It's most important to keep our eyes focused on God in everything we say and do.

As the song mentions, we can do our best to keep our eyes focused on God and His plan for our lives. God knows that we will fall and make mistakes, but He also knows we are trying our best. He doesn't think any less of us when we wander from Him, but He is so happy when we return to Him full-heartedly. If we'd gain the whole world, we would lose our souls, and it's better to have our souls gain eternity in heaven. With Jesus, there will be no more pain or sorrow. Who wouldn't want our souls to gain eternity in heaven?

1. What would it mean for me to gain the world and lose my soul?

____

____

____

____

____

2. What steps can I take to ensure that I don't lose my soul and stay focused on God?

____

____

____

____

____

Dear God, please help me to keep my mind, body, and soul focused on you in everything I do. Help me to remember that it only benefits me to keep my life focused on you because I'll get to have eternity in heaven with you. Please help me to bring others to you and to help my family and friends stay focused on you. In Jesus' name, amen.

Day 65
Created for God's Glory

"Everyone who is called by my name, whom I created
for my glory, whom I formed and made."
Isaiah 43:7

God made everything and every one of us with His own specific needs in mind. I want to live my life to the fullest to glorify God in everything I say and do. I want others to see the change in me and to come up and ask me, "what do you have inside you, man?" "Why are you so happy? How do you have so much peace in almost any situation?" Then I get the honor and privilege of telling them how Jesus changed my life. I get to tell everyone who may be seeking their purpose that they are all called by His name and for His glory. He will help them find their true purpose just like He did with me. It's an honor that He chose and called me for His glory.

Just like this man helps people find their God-given purpose in their lives, we, too, can help people find their purpose. Being called by His glory and for His purpose means living our lives for Him every day. It means fighting through challenges and trials and being able to praise Him in both good times and bad. We can see it as an honor that He chose us for His glory.

1. How can I use my life to glorify and honor God?

____

____

____

____

____

2. Do I really believe that I'm made by God and for God's glory?

____

____

____

____

____

Dear God, thank you for calling me to your grand assignment even before I was born. Thank you for creating me for your purpose. Thank you that I'm called by your name. Help me to know my calling and enjoy it every day. In Jesus' name, amen.

Day 66
Confess Our Sins

"Therefore, confess your sins to one another and pray
for one another, that you may be healed. The prayer of
a righteous person has great power as it is working."
James 5:16

I used to not have the greatest relationship with my dad. But as I got older, I realized how much I longed to be closer to him. After I'd accepted Jesus as my Lord and Savior, I knew I wanted to try to get closer to my dad. One day, after a lot of prayer and thoughts, I built up the courage to talk to him one on one with no one else around about our relationship and where it was going. I told him I wanted to know him better as his son. I apologized for how I acted toward him over the years, and he apologized to me for how he acted towards me. We learned to forgive each other, and now through God's help, I have a much better relationship with him today. We each confessed our thoughts about our relationship and were able to be completely honest with each other. God helped us work on our relationship.

Just like God helped this son and his father mend their relationship, He can help us mend any relationship with people. Whether we have a grievance against our wife, our children, or someone from work, we can go to that person and tell them how sorry we are for our actions. We can offer to pray for them and with them if they let us. All we can do is be completely honest and ask for their forgiveness. The prayer of a righteous person works and has great power.

1. Am I willing to confess any sins I've committed against people, whether in thought, word, or deed?

2. What can I do to repair any lost connections with the people I care about?

Dear God, please allow me to mend any relationships that are strained in my life with your help. Help me to speak your words in each of those situations, not my own. Thank you for the opportunity to mend the relationships that you've wanted me to mend. Help me to be calm and forgive people quickly. In Jesus' name, amen.

DAY 67

PRAYER OF FAITH

"And the prayer of faith will save the one who
is sick, and the Lord will raise him up. And if he
has committed sins, he will be forgiven."
JAMES 5:15

James, one of the apostles of Jesus, wrote the book named after him. He followed Jesus and helped people come to know Jesus as their Lord and Savior. James wanted to help others know that they could be forgiven for their sins and that they could even ask for forgiveness from the other people they'd hurt in their past. The prayer of faith will help save the ones who are sick. The disciples prayed many times for sick people following Jesus and even after He ascended into heaven. The Lord would heal those He chooses to heal and raise them to eternity with Him. This verse reminds everyone that if they are truly sorry and ask for forgiveness, they will be forgiven.

We can take this verse to heart and ask for forgiveness from anyone that we wronged in our lives. It takes courage to ask God and others we have wronged for forgiveness. Some people we ask for forgiveness may not want to forgive us now, later, or ever. But God wants us to return to Him and restart a relationship with Him at any time. He also wants us to go to others and ask for their forgiveness no matter what their reaction is to us. Jesus will forgive us for our sins even if the people we talk to don't forgive us.

1. Do I really believe in the prayer of faith in my life?

____

____

____

____

____

2. What can I do to start praying over my life, goals, and dreams in faith that God has already given me?

____

____

____

____

____

Dear God, please help me to lead a life that is pleasing to you. Help me to live in faith and to come to you in prayer first, instead of last every day. Help me to want to pray every day to keep the light of faith in my heart in every situation. In Jesus' name, amen.

DAY 68
ABUNDANCE OF PROSPERITY AND SECURITY

"Behold, I will bring to it health and healing,
and I will heal them and reveal to them
abundance of prosperity and security."
JEREMIAH 33:6

Jesus promises everyone that He will bring healing to everyone and everything. Look at how many men, women, and children He healed. He even dined with Zacchaeus, who was a hated tax collector. He made a point to say, "Zacchaeus, I am going to your house today." Even though people made a point to tell Him not to go to Zacchaeus's house, Zacchaeus gladly accepted Jesus' invitation. They told Him that whatever he had cheated people out of, he would pay them back many more times the amount. Jesus changed Zacchaeus's life and other men's lives in miraculous ways. Look at the crippled man who was dropped into the house that Jesus was in by his friends. Jesus healed him, and he told him to get up and walk. All at once, he was healed by Jesus' mercy and grace.

Jesus offers to heal us and give us abundant life with our families daily. All we have to do is accept His healing over our lives, whether in our relationships with our wives, daughters, mothers, grandparents, aunts, uncles, or even people at work. He wants us to be abundantly blessed and filled with prosperity throughout our lives. Whatever we struggle with, we can come before God, asking for healing for our souls and bodies. There is nothing He won't do for us as His beloved sons.

1. Do I really believe that God will bring me abundant life and help me to have security and prosperity?

2. In what ways can I spread the good news to others that God wants to bless them with abundance and prosperity in their lives?

Dear God, please help me to believe with all my heart that I will receive health, healing, abundance, and prosperity. Thank you that I can come to you whenever I need to, whether or not I feel worthy of being in your presence. Thank you for blessing me with supernatural healing, even if I don't see it or feel it right away. In Jesus' name, amen.

DAY 69
GOD STRETCHED OUT HIS HAND

"While you stretch out your hand to heal, and
signs and wonders are performed through
the name of your holy servant Jesus."
ACTS 4:30

Peter and John were two of the disciples that were able to heal many people in the name of Jesus by His power and His power alone. Even when they were both seized and put in jail, they were still praising God and marveling at the miracles that He had helped them do. They still firmly believed that they would be rescued from their predicament in jail by the Lord Himself and that there would be many more miracles, signs, and wonders they could perform for the people through Jesus and Jesus alone. They knew to give credit where it was ultimately due, and they had no problem proclaiming the goodness of God even from their prison cells.

We can give credit to Jesus for any healing that we receive from God from any illness or sickness, whether mental, physical, emotional, or spiritual. We also know to praise God continually for our friends and family when anyone in our lives receives healing. Jesus is the ultimate great physician. Our healing and our families' healing didn't come from anything we did physically. Yes, we prayed and believed for healing and didn't give up hope that healing would be miraculously brought on. Still, we also knew it was not us bringing about the healing. Rather, Jesus brought about the healing because of His mercy and grace.

1. Do I believe that the signs and wonders Peter and John were referring to were true?

____

____

____

____

____

2. What can I do to help people in my life believe that the signs and miracles that Peter and John performed were true?

____

____

____

____

____

Dear God, please help me to help people know you on a deeply personal level. Please help them realize that the signs and wonders that you talked about in the Bible were actually real. Thank you that every miracle was a sign of your love and devotion to your children. In Jesus' name, amen.

Day 70

Healing

Jesus had no fear when He preached His Father's Gospel. He taught in the synagogues when He was young, from when He was 30 until He was 33. He boldly went everywhere the Father told Him to go and healed many people with debilitating sicknesses and illnesses. It must have been incredible for people to be up close and personal with Jesus and to have Him heal them from demon possessions and what they thought were never-ending diseases. People must have been so amazed at what Jesus could do. He proclaimed the Good News, all the while knowing that He had to eventually suffer death on the cross to save everyone on earth. He healed lepers, turned water into wine, walked on water, and cast demons out of people. There was nothing He couldn't do.

We can have healing from God in our lives. All we have to do is believe that we will receive full healing and that anyone in our families will receive full healing from Jesus. We can tell others that they can receive healing from everything they are suffering from, whether it's work stress, school stress, family stress, or anything else that could be happening to them. We can offer to pray for and with anyone who approaches us and needs a listening ear because they are going through a hard time. We can be there for them and help them feel better mentally, emotionally, and spiritually.

1. How can I ask God to bring about healing for other people who need it and me?

____

____

____

____

____

2. What specifics can I ask for in terms of healing for me, my friends, and my family?

____

____

____

____

____

Dear God, please help me to bring whatever healing needs I have to you. Please help me to believe that I will be healed. Please help me to pray for others who need healing and give me your eyes to their specific needs. Thank you that I get to pray your thoughts over their lives and bodies, not mine. In Jesus' name, amen.

Day 71

Live in Harmony

"Live in harmony with one another. Do not be haughty, but associate with the lowly. Never be wise in your own sight. Repay no one evil for evil, but give thought to do what is honorable in the sight of all. If possible, so far as it depends on you, live peaceably with all."

Romans 12:16-18

Even when Peter and John were imprisoned, they did what was honorable in God's sight. They worshiped and praised Him despite their circumstances. They lived in as much harmony as possible with the other prisoners while sharing the gospel. They knew better than to think too highly of themselves and knew it was their job to spread God's truth through every trial and trouble. They didn't think too highly of themselves because they knew they were doing the right thing for God. They didn't have to repay evil for evil. They made every effort to live in peace with everyone around them.

Just like Peter and John lived in peace with people in prison and all around the towns where they went, we too can make every effort to live in peace with the people around us. We can open the door for strangers, help carry people's grocery bags, and just be kind to everyone we meet. We don't need to start meaningless dramas or arguments with people we might disagree with. But instead, we can let people have their opinion just like we have our opinions. We can also live in harmony with nature and ensure we care for the environment.

1. How can I live peacefully throughout my life?

____

____

____

____

____

2. What can I do to not think too highly of myself?

____

____

____

____

____

Dear God, please help me to not think highly of myself. Help me to live in peace and harmony with everyone I meet and to treat them as you would treat them. Help me to live an honorable life that brings glory to you in everything I think, say, and do. In Jesus' name, amen.

DAY 72

PUT ON LOVE

*"And above all this put-on love, which binds
everything together in perfect harmony."*
COLOSSIANS 3:14

Jesus was the truest and purest example of humbleness and love. He came to earth as a baby, was born in a manger, and then He had His ministry for three years, where He went from town to town and city to city proclaiming His Father's Good News. He had love in His heart for all people, and He never stopped loving everyone even though they were all sinners in need of His mercy, grace, and forgiveness. Even when the guards and Judas came to take Him away, He didn't fight back. When He was questioned, He didn't talk back. He lived in harmony with everyone.

We can follow Jesus' example and live in harmony with the people in our lives. When our wives or girlfriends ask us to do something, we can do it gladly without complaining. When our kids want to play basketball with us, we can make time for them. If our wives or girlfriends tell us they want to spend more time with us, we can make time for a date night. When our boss asks us to finish an important project before the end of the week, we can do our best to finish it before the deadline without complaining about how much work it is for us. It is hard to show love in every situation, but it is worth it because we follow Jesus' example.

1. How can I live in harmony with people?

____

____

____

____

2. In what ways can I put on love?

____

____

____

____

Dear God, please help me to show love to everyone in my life and help me to live in harmony with people. Help me to remember that love binds us all together. Thank you for always showing me true love. Help me to live in love no matter how I feel or what I may be going through. In Jesus' name, amen.

Day 73
Brothers Dwell in Unity

"Behold, how good and pleasant it is
when brothers dwell in unity!"
Psalm 133:1

Remember the story of Joseph? He got sold into slavery by his brothers because of their overwhelming jealousy of him being Jacob's favorite son. But later, he was named second in command behind Pharaoh. His brothers came to Egypt because of the famine in Cana. Egypt was the only place that had food available. When Joseph saw his brothers again, at first, he wanted to get back at them for betraying him. But God eventually softened his heart, and Joseph told them he wouldn't harm any of them because he was their brother. He invited them to be his guests and lived in unity with them.

Brothers who dwell in unity every chance they get are better off than brothers who quarrel every chance. We can try our best to be nice to everyone we contact, whether they are nice to us or not. God clarifies that it's pleasant and good when brothers get along. Just like Joseph finally got along with his brothers, we can be quick to forgive our brothers and ask for their forgiveness for the things we've done wrong.

1. How am I dwelling with my brothers in unity every day?

____

____

____

____

____

2. In what ways can I be more pleasant to my brothers every day?

____

____

____

____

____

Dear God, please help me to be pleasant to be around at work, at home, and with my children and wife. Please help me to dwell in unity with everyone in my life as You dwelled in unity with people. Give me the ability to let the little things go and to enjoy life. In Jesus' name, amen.

Day 74

Be United in Our Minds

"I appeal to you, brothers, by the name of our Lord
Jesus Christ, that all of you agree, and that there
be no divisions among you, but that you be united
in the same mind and the same judgment."
1 Corinthians 1:10

Whenever there was any division between my brother and me, I would always try to be the first one to apologize to him. My parents raised me to be the first one to apologize to anyone, whether they were willing to forgive me or not. There's nothing more important than family staying close to one another. Even when I have disagreements with my wife, as every couple has, she and I always talk things through and try our best to never go to bed angry. We have never given up on our marriage vows. Amazingly, we have been married for more than 35 years and have known each other for 43 years. We try daily to be united with God and each other in love.

When there is division among people, there are arguments. Even though it can be tempting to speak our minds with our brothers, friends, and families, it is more important to keep our mouths shut instead of creating drama or adversity between our families or us. We can agree to disagree with people in our lives without starting arguments. We should try our best to live in unity and agree with our wives daily.

1. How am I united under the same judgment and in the same mindset as my spouse?

2. What can I do to be united with my spouse every day?

Dear God, please help me to honor my spouse and come to an agreement with her even though it's hard sometimes. Help us to be united as one mind through your power and love. Thank you for the ability to be united with you and my wife as one every day. In Jesus' name, amen.

DAY 75
DO GOOD TO EVERYONE

"So then, as we have opportunity, let us do
good to everyone, and especially to those
who are of the household of faith."
GALATIANS 6:10

The kids next door always help us shovel the snow whenever the weather turns. They are very nice kids who always help us, whether helping us shovel or any other housework we need. They help other people on the street. It gives us a great opportunity to tell them about Jesus whenever they spend time with us. Their parents taught them to do nice things for the people they spend time with. Even if we don't tell them about Jesus, we enjoy spending time with them when they offer to help us.

Just like this man's neighbors help him and do good things for him when he needs help, Jesus tells us to do good to the people around us. We can help others do good to those around us, especially our brothers and sisters in Christ. We can engage with people in weekly Bible studies, prayers, and being present with them. Doing good makes us feel good because we are helping others feel good.

1. Am I doing good to those close to me in the faith?

____

____

____

____

____

2. What steps can I take to do better for those in their faith walk?

____

____

____

____

____

Dear God, please help me to do good to those around me no matter how I may be feeling on any given day. Help me to do good to those who know you and especially to those who don't know you. Let me seek out every opportunity and lead me to new opportunities to do good to people and for people. In Jesus' name, amen.

Day 76

By Grace, You've Been Saved

"For it is by grace you have been saved, through faith—and this is not from yourselves, it is the gift of God— ⁹not by works, so that no one can boast."
Ephesians 2:8-9

My mom had gotten into an accident and fractured her neck. She was miraculously not paralyzed. She was 88 years old and ended up having a lot of complications from the accident. We moved her from the hospital to a rehab facility and back to the hospital in the middle of covid. We weren't able to see her a lot because of the restrictions. I prayed for her to receive miraculous healing and believed God would heal her. My mom believed in Jesus and knew she would be reunited with my dad in heaven. I was sad that He didn't heal her on earth, but we did hear her recite the Apostles Creed from memory when she was under heavy sedation with morphine. It proved to me that God was taking care of her. She died on my wife's and my 34th wedding anniversary, but we were honored that she was united with Jesus on our day.

Just like this man prayed for healing for his mother, we, too, pray for healing for our family members whenever they have accidents or are sick. Our prayers are the things that carry us through the hard times. God gives us the strength to keep praying even when we may not know what to pray for. We can keep believing that God will heal our family members even if it's not on earth. They will be healed and made whole in heaven.

"

1. Have I been praying faithfully for anyone who is sick in my life?

2. What can I do to help the people who are sick in my life and believe in the power of prayer?

Dear God, please help me to believe in the power of prayer. Please help heal the people who need it the most. Thank you for the reminder that I am saved by faith, not by works. Thank you for saving me through the free gift of salvation. In Jesus' name, amen.

Day 77

God's Power is Better Than Human Wisdom

"so that your faith might not rest on human
wisdom, but on God's power."
1 Corinthians 2:5

When Joseph was given power over all of Egypt and was second in command under Pharaoh, he didn't take advantage of his power. He interpreted the dream Pharaoh had about the sickly cows and withered grain and helped everyone develop a plan to help keep food in Egypt even during the famine. He used his unique gifts to everyone's advantage. He used his power wisely and helped people not go hungry. He didn't let his faith rest on what he could do. Rather, he let his faith rest on God's power. He knew that God's ultimate power rested on his life and that God had a plan for him. He let God's power work instead of thinking he automatically knew everything.

As men, we tend to get overzealous and want to take credit for our own wisdom. Still, God gives us the wisdom to act correctly in every situation. He helps us know what actions to take in any and every situation. All we have to do is ask Him for the wisdom we need. When we struggle with knowing which path to take for college, we can ask Him to guide us on what major we should take. When we are starting to tell our kids about Jesus, we can ask Him to help us speak to the kids on their personal level. When a friend asks for advice, we can ask God whether we should give advice or just sit and listen to them.

1. Where does my faith rest- in myself or in God alone?

2. What can I do to stop thinking that I can have wisdom on my own instead of asking God for wisdom?

Dear God, please help me to not think that my wisdom only comes through my own power and knowledge. Please help me to remember that my wisdom comes from you alone. Thank you for your power. In Jesus' name, amen.

DAY 78
INCREASE OUR FAITH

"The apostles said to the Lord, "Increase our faith!"
⁶ He replied, "If you have faith as small as a mustard
seed, you can say to this mulberry tree, 'Be uprooted
and planted in the sea,' and it will obey you."
LUKE 17:5-7

The disciples wanted their faith to be increased, and all they had to do was look to Jesus. They were with Him almost every day in His three-year ministry. So, their faith must have increased every time they were around Him, especially after seeing Him perform so many miracles, signs, and wonders. Even when He rose from the dead and appeared in the upper room, they must have been floored that He was in front of them again. When He allowed the tongues of fire to rest on the disciples and allowed them to speak in many different languages, they probably had no doubt in God's power. No one had the first-hand experience of being His disciples like them. He told them if they had faith as small as a mustard seed, it would make a tremendous difference.

We can be like the disciples and ask God to increase our faith through our everyday situations, including college, time with our families, taking our kids to school, to spending time with our spouses. We can have our faith increased when we go through difficult situations and come out even stronger on the other side. God tells us the same thing: we can increase our faith by keeping our faith strong in Him alone. Whenever we think we won't be able to do something, that is when we can remember that our faith can always change our circumstances.

"

1. How can I get and keep my faith strong even through hard times?

2. What can I do to increase my faith every day?

Dear God, please help me to keep my faith strong even in the midst of adversity. Thank you for reminding me to keep the faith even when I feel like I have very little left to give. Please help me to help others know how to keep the faith. In Jesus' name, amen.

Day 79

Overcome the World

"For everyone born of God overcomes the world. This is
the victory that has overcome the world, even our faith."
1 John 5:4

In The Lion King, Simba realizes he is the rightful king of pride rock. He realizes he is truly Mufasa's son and needs to take his rightful place as king. Even though his uncle Scar had taken Mufasa's place as king, his father appeared to him in the clouds and said, "remember who you are." He knew right then he had to go back and face his past, even though he had been running from it for so long. Simba fought Scar and won the victory that was rightfully his, to begin with. After defeating Scar, Simba was crowned king of pride rock.

Everyone born of God can take their rightful places in their lives and do what He has called them to do. Through Him, we have victory. God may not appear in the clouds as Mufasa did to Simba, but He does make His presence known to us in many different ways. These include talking to us in our dreams, guiding us through life with promptings from the Holy Spirit, and telling us what is right and wrong. He tells us when to be quiet and when to speak out. He also tells us to remember who we are, His beloved children.

1. How can I help people who don't know God come to know Him personally?

____

____

____

____

2. What can I do to keep the faith in my own life?

____

____

____

____

____

Dear God, please help me to overcome the pressures and stressors of this world through faith. Help me to bring others to know you through my faith and through my thoughts, words, and actions. Please remind me that the victory is already mine through my faith. Whenever I get discouraged, please remind me who I am. In Jesus' name, amen.

Day 80
Testing of Our Faith

"For you know that the testing of your
faith produces steadfastness."
James 1:3

Able was the brother of Cain and the son of Adam and Eve. Able was a shepherd, and he was noble and brought sacrifices of his flock that pleased God. Cain, his brother, was very jealous of him and killed him. God then asked him where his brother was, and Cain said, "am I my brother's keeper?" Then God sent him into the wilderness but still had favor on him so no one would ever try to kill him or try to harm him. Even if anyone threatened to harm him, they wouldn't succeed because God was always with him.

Cain didn't fully lose his relationship with God even though God tested his faith. The Bible says that testing our faith produces perseverance, and everything we go through can bring us closer to God instead of pushing us away from God. Every test can bring us to the realization that God is healing us through whatever we go through. The testing of our faith produces perseverance and steadfastness. We can turn to God no matter how we feel or are doing. He wants us to come before Him when we are being tested and tell Him what we are dealing with and going through. He wants us to admit that we need help from Him every day.

1. How has my faith been tested?

____

____

____

____

____

2. What things can I do when my faith gets tested, and how can I have perseverance?

____

____

____

____

____

Dear God, please help me to stay strong in the midst of adversity. I know that your word says that the testing of my faith produces perseverance. Help me to face challenges head-on with your unconditional love and support in every situation. Thank you that I can turn to you at any time for help. In Jesus' name, amen.

Day 81
Sanctified by Truth

"Sanctify them by the truth; your word is truth."
John 17:17

During high school, I went to a Bible study with my friends. While there, the pastor asked anyone who wanted to commit their life to Christ. I heard God tell me to go to the altar and ask Jesus to come back into my life. I told Him that I was sorry for walking away from Him. My friends put their hands on me as I kneeled on the altar. As soon as I asked Jesus into my life again, a surreal peace washed over me. That's when I knew God was working on my heart and life.

Just like this man asked Jesus to come back into his life, we can ask Him to come back into our lives whenever we wander astray. Jesus tells us that His Word is the truth and that we should sanctify everyone with the truth of His word. Nothing is more important than helping those who have wandered return to Him. Whether it's someone we know or just met, we can meet them right where they are and share God's love with them. Sanctifying them with God's truth can save their lives and help them realize what they are missing. We can even look back at our lives and see where we had gone wrong. We can ask for forgiveness and tell God we want Him back in our hearts and lives. He will willingly accept us back no matter what we have done.

1. How have I been sanctified through my relationship with Christ?

____

____

____

____

____

2. In what ways can I tell others that they, too, can be sanctified through Christ even though they sin?

____

____

____

____

____

Dear God, please help me to turn back to you every time I am led astray by this world. Please help me to let others know of your promise and the sanctification of your truth. Please guide me to say and do the right things to lead others to know you personally. In Jesus' name, amen.

DAY 82
DENY OURSELVES

Peter, James, John, and all other disciples were told to pick up their cross daily and follow Him. Look at Daniel. He denied King Darius because he wanted Daniel to worship him. Rather than denying God, Daniel kept his eyes focused on God at all times. When Peter denied Jesus three times, he was so ashamed, but Jesus forgave him. When John was taken into prison, he kept his focus on God, denied himself, and followed Jesus all his life. Think about it, John followed Jesus even before Jesus was even alive. John was preaching about Him and told people to repent, for He was near. John picked up his cross and followed Jesus throughout his life. Abraham followed Jesus all the days of his life to the point where he almost sacrificed his only son, Isaac but God provided a ram instead of having Isaac be sacrificed.

If all of those men can pick up their crosses daily in their lives and follow Jesus, we, too, can pick up our crosses and follow Him. Whenever we struggle to give up ourselves, we can ask God to help us trust Him with every aspect of our lives, even unto death when we get called home. If we want to be His disciples, we have to give up and say, "Lord, please help me follow you and enjoy bringing others to know you through my thoughts, words, and actions."

1. How have I denied myself and picked up my cross daily to follow Jesus?

2. In what ways can I take up my cross and follow Him?

Dear God, please help me to deny myself and follow you daily, no matter how hard it can be. Help me to know the different ways I can deny myself and impact the world with your unconditional love and your important truth. Thank you for the opportunity to deny myself and follow You. In Jesus' name, amen.

Day 83

It Will Be Done unto Us

Bible verse: "If you remain in me and my words remain in you, ask whatever you wish, and it will be done for you."
John 15:7

Most people have probably heard the story of Job. Even though he faced insurmountable odds, he never stopped praising God. He lost his crops, friends, and family and even had painful sores on his body. He went through so much turmoil and pain in his life that when we look at his story, we are amazed that he even chose to keep his faith and believe in God the way he did. Those circumstances would probably make anyone feel like turning away from God. Not to mention, all those circumstances hit him right after the other. But instead of turning away from God, Job remained close to God and believed that he would receive healing, strength, and perseverance. Job continued walking with God and saw His faithfulness in every circumstance.

Remaining in God and His Word is hard because we have daily distractions, and we sin even though we don't always mean to. We even let unwholesome thoughts and words come out of our mouths. We walk away from God because of the distractions in this world. God tells us to remain close to Him to see the fullness of His love and the restoration He can bring to our lives.

1. How can I remain in God and have God remain in me physically, mentally, and emotionally?

____

____

____

____

____

2. What do I need to ask in Jesus' name to remain in God, whether spiritual, emotional, or physical healing?

____

____

____

____

____

Dear God, please help me to remain in you and to keep your words in my heart at all times. Help me to be bold and ask for things that I need and even long for. Help me to believe that I will receive whatever I ask for through your power. In Jesus' name, amen.

Day 84
Belief in Jesus

"While Jesus was still speaking, some people came
from the house of Jairus, the synagogue leader.
"Your daughter is dead," they said. "Why bother
the teacher anymore." Overhearing what they said,
Jesus told him, "Don't be afraid; just believe."
Mark 5:35-36

In this story, a man named Jairus went to Jesus to ask, nonetheless beg, for healing for his daughter. He asked Jesus to come to his house and heal her. Jesus was willing to help anyone who needed Him. People didn't want Jairus to bother Jesus because his daughter was dead. Jesus heard what they were saying and told everyone there to believe. In another translation, it even said Jesus ignored what they were saying. So, if anyone gets a bad report from the doctor, we can ignore it because if Jesus can heal Jairus's daughter, He too can heal our hearts and lives. It doesn't mean not hearing what the doctor is saying and taking his or her advice, but we can rest assured that no matter what we go through, God already has the final say in our lives. His plan was, is, and forever will be good, and He has hope and a purpose for us.

We can ignore the naysayers when they say anything against our lives. We don't have to let their words affect our feelings, minds, or physical bodies. Instead, we can meditate on and believe fully in the promises of God every day. We don't have to worry about burdening God because He is never burdened by us. He wants to know us. Even though He knows everything on our minds, He wants us to trust Him enough to confide in Him.

1. How can I help others believe in and see the glory of God?

____

____

____

____

____

2. What can I do to remind myself to believe that I never burden Jesus?

____

____

____

____

____

Dear God, please help me to know you in everything I say and do. Please help me to believe in you and your power no matter what is happening in my life. Thank you for allowing me to help others to believe in your goodness. In Jesus' name, amen.

Day 85

Keep His Commands

"In fact, this is love for God: to keep his commands.
And his commands are not burdensome."
1 John 5:3

Even though every man in the Bible sinned, they repented for their sins and asked Him for forgiveness. God wanted them to know Him on a deeply personal level. Even though it was difficult for them to keep His commands at certain times, God already knew they would fall short every day. He didn't hold sins against any man in the Bible. Even though the men in the Bible were burdened by the things going on in their lives, they could come to God and tell Him exactly what they were feeling.

The commands that God gives His people are not to be considered burdensome. He gave us His commandments, so we know what to do and what not to do. They aren't just rules that annoy us daily, but they can help us learn how to live lives pleasing to Him. Instead of seeing the commandments as annoying, we can see them as challenges to learning how to be close to God daily. We love God when we keep His commands. They teach us how to live in harmony with everyone around us. He gave us the commands in His word to teach us how to love Him and others. His commands are not supposed to be burdensome. They are supposed to be something we enjoy doing every day.

1. How can I come to God and believe that I'm not burdening Him?

____

____

____

____

____

2. In what ways do I feel like I'm burdening God?

____

____

____

____

____

Dear God, please help me to not see your commands as burdensome. Help me to love you, believe in your promises, and meditate on them every day. Help me to help others who see your commands as burdensome to see your commands as privileges to become closer to you. In Jesus' name, amen.

Day 86
Gaining a Heart of Wisdom

"Teach us to number our days, that we
may gain a heart of wisdom."
Psalm 90:12

I want to live a life pleasing to God and help others know Him in the same way I do. I didn't know Him personally until I was in my thirties. I went through the traumatic experience of almost losing my daughter. Now, I talk to Him every day without fail and ask Him to protect my family. I ask Him to help me gain wisdom that can only come from knowing Him, so I can share His goodness with the world. If I see someone struggling, I offer encouragement to them, and if I see someone who has lost someone they love, I tell them that they can see them again when they get to heaven. People ask me why I'm so happy, and I get the opportunity to tell them about God and the difference He made in my life.

Everyone knows their days are numbered, and we must do our best to gain as much Godly wisdom as possible. Knowing Jesus as our Lord and Savior is the most important thing we can ever do. God wants us to know what He can and will do for us when we turn our lives over and trust Him fully. We can help our families, friends, and coworkers to know Jesus. We can also help them gain Godly wisdom in every area of their lives.

1. How do I fill my heart with wisdom?

2. In what ways can I help others gain wisdom about God and number our days wisely?

Dear God, please help me to remember that my days are numbered and to live my life for you. Help me gain a heart that is full of wisdom in ways that only you can. Thank you for always being here for me. Thank you for helping me understand your wisdom and what it means for my life. In Jesus' name, amen.

Day 87
Bringing Calm

"Fools give full vent to their rage,
but the wise bring calm in the end."
Proverbs 29:11

Every man has times when he gets very angry. Even Jesus got angry at the tax collectors for collecting money in His father's house. He actually threw the tables across the church and scattered all of the money all over the floor and across the church. We don't have to worry if we feel angry over something that happened to us because even Jesus had moments of anger.

There is no emotion that Jesus hasn't felt, just like all of us. When we get angry, we can ask God to help us not stay in those angry moods because it will only destroy us mentally and emotionally if we stay angry for too long. Holding on to anger and rage only causes us physical problems, too, like heart and stomach problems. If we are mad at our spouses over a disagreement, we can wait until we calm down and talk to them when we can think rationally. If we are mad at our children for a mistake they made, we can approach them with love and help them understand how to change their behavior. If someone makes a mistake at work, we can calmly correct it in ways they can understand.

1. How can I stop venting and stay calm no matter the circumstances?

____

____

____

____

____

2. In what ways can I help others keep from venting and instead help them stay calm?

____

____

____

____

____

Dear God, please take away any rage that I might be feeling inside me. Help me to remember that even Jesus got angry. Please help me to remember that a fool gives full vent to their rage, but through You, I can stay calm in every situation. In Jesus' name, amen.

DAY 88

KNOWLEDGE OF GOD

"Oh, the depth of the riches of the wisdom and
knowledge of God! How unsearchable his
judgments, and his paths beyond tracing out!"
ROMANS 11:33

David knew that God's ways were unchangeable and unsearchable. God knew that David would go through all of his trials even before he was born, and God knew exactly how to help him through them. When he was persecuted and pursued by Saul, God made it so Saul wouldn't be able to harm David. When he had the affair with Bathsheba, God delivered him from that mistake and showed him a favor. He asked God to fill him with His heavenly wisdom instead of earthly wisdom, and David became one of the Godliest kings on earth.

God's ways are unsearchable, and His wisdom is beyond anyone's ability to know. He plans every day of our lives and wants us to enjoy our lives to the fullest. Whenever we don't understand something, we can come to Him and ask Him about it without fear or reproach. We don't have to know everything there is to know. We don't have to think too highly of ourselves when God gives us the wisdom we have wanted for a long time. Rather, when we get that wisdom, we can thank God for giving it to us.

1. How can I remind myself that God's ways of wisdom and knowledge are unsearchable?

2. In what ways can I help people know about the goodness of God's wisdom?

Dear God, please help me to remember that your ways are more amazing than mine. Whenever I think I might know the best paths to take, please remind me that your knowledge about my life is more than I could ever understand. Help me to trust your plans no matter where they take me. In Jesus' name, amen.

Day 89
Understanding None Can Fathom

"Do you not know? Have you not heard? The
LORD is the everlasting God, the Creator of the
ends of the earth. He will not grow tired or weary,
and his understanding no one can fathom."
Isaiah 40:28

In the story of the prodigal son, the son wanted and got his inheritance from his father and spent it all frivolously. Once he realized he had no money or food, he was afraid to return to his dad and ask him for forgiveness. He was so ashamed and hungry that he wanted to eat the scraps that the pigs were eating. He went back to his father's house, and the father accepted him with unconditional love. Even though his son had made mistakes and grown tired and weary, the father never gave up on praying for his son.

It can bring us much comfort to know that God will never grow tired or weary, even when we grow tired and weary. Just like the prodigal son's father never gave up on praying for his son, Jesus never grows tired of interceding on our behalf. He never grows tired of listening to us, no matter how we are feeling or what we have on our minds. We can come to Him in prayer at any time, no matter what. Even though we will never know how everything will turn out on earth, He knows how everything will turn out.

1. How can I remind myself that God will never grow weary at any time?

2. In what ways can I remind my wife and/or children that God is the everlasting God?

Dear God, thank you for being the most important person in my life. Please help me spread your words of wisdom and knowledge to my children, wife, my coworkers, and anyone I come in contact with. Please help me to spread the news that you are the everlasting God anywhere you want me to go. In Jesus' name, amen.

DAY 90
WITH WISDOM, THERE IS A FUTURE

"Know also that wisdom is like honey for you.
If you find it, there is a future hope for you,
and your hope will not be cut off."
PROVERBS 24:14

David prayed for his infant son to be healed even after he had sinned and had an affair with Bathsheba. David prayed for the wisdom of Jesus to fill his heart. Even though his son didn't survive, he still praised God for forgiving him of his sins and delivering his son from a difficult earthly life. He knew he would see his son again in heaven one day.

When we go through health issues such as cancer, diabetes, dialysis, covid, and many other forms of illness, we can remember that God is always with us. We can ask Him for the wisdom to help us, our spouses, children, and friends, through any illness we go through. We can encourage them when they feel like giving up and remind them that God has a wonderful plan for their lives that He will help them fulfill. When we see one of them struggling, we can pray with them, asking God to give them wisdom as to what doctors they should go to, what specialists to see, and what hospital they should go to. Worldly wisdom will only make us feel more confused and skeptical about the decisions we have to make. But Godly wisdom will make us certain without a shadow of a doubt that we are making the right choice. Just like David, we can rest in God's promise to give us the wisdom we need in every situation, especially in the middle of a medical diagnosis.

1. How can I obtain more wisdom in my relationship with Christ every day?

____

____

____

____

____

2. In what ways can I help others believe that they can obtain wisdom through their relationship with God?

____

____

____

____

____

Dear God, please help me to spread much-needed wisdom about you to the people that mean the most to me. Help me not be afraid to spread your words of wisdom to strangers if the opportunity arises. Help me to turn to you for wisdom about what paths I should take if a friend, family member, or myself gets an unfortunate medical diagnosis. In Jesus' name, amen.

Conclusion

I hope you have learned how to follow God more daily by reading this 90-day devotional. I also hope you have learned how to be a better husband, father, grandpa, friend, worker, and a man who follows God with all your heart.

I hope you learned how to be there for your wife and/or girlfriend in the way God wants you to be there for her and that you have learned to cherish, honor, and protect her.

Do everything you can to help your wife or girlfriend through difficult times with tenderness and love. I hope you have learned how to be there for your children and even your grandchildren and to approach things in their lives on their own individual levels.

I also hope you can lead everyone in your life closer to God through your words and actions. Whenever your children, wife, or friends want to talk, listen to them without giving them advice. Remember, sometimes they just need someone to listen to them. At work, I hope you can honor your bosses and enjoy your job to the fullest with God's help. Remember, your family is the dream of the lonely, and your job is the dream of the jobless.

You can ask God to help you do everything you can to make sure your family life and work life are balanced and thrive simultaneously. God will never leave you or forsake you. May God help you be present in every situation and be the leader God called you to be in your family.